基于重要性和表现维度的
中国创意文化产业区分析

An Importance-Performance Analysis of Creative Culture Industry District in China

张雪松／著

经济管理出版社
ECONOMY & MANAGEMENT PUBLISHING HOUSE

图书在版编目（CIP）数据

基于重要性和表现维度的中国创意文化产业区分析/张雪松著．—北京：经济管理出版社，2018.8
ISBN 978-7-5096-5920-5

Ⅰ.①基… Ⅱ.①张… Ⅲ.①文化产业—商业区—研究—中国 Ⅳ.①G124

中国版本图书馆 CIP 数据核字（2018）第 169644 号

组稿编辑：张巧梅
责任编辑：张巧梅
责任印制：黄章平
责任校对：赵天宇

出版发行：经济管理出版社
（北京市海淀区北蜂窝 8 号中雅大厦 A 座 11 层　100038）
网　　址：www.E-mp.com.cn
电　　话：（010）51915602
印　　刷：北京玺诚印务有限公司
经　　销：新华书店
开　　本：720mm×1000mm/16
印　　张：8.5
字　　数：158 千字
版　　次：2018 年 9 月第 1 版　2018 年 9 月第 1 次印刷
书　　号：ISBN 978-7-5096-5920-5
定　　价：58.00 元

·版权所有　翻印必究·
凡购本社图书，如有印装错误，由本社读者服务部负责调换。
联系地址：北京阜外月坛北小街 2 号
电话：（010）68022974　　邮编：100836

Abstract

This dissertation mainly focuses on analyzing the growing phenomena of creative culture districts in China through studying and analyzing cases. By not only studying the typical cases of seven – nine – eight creative culture districts in domestic, but also identifying two successful cases of Philadelphia's culture districts in America and Insa – Dong culture district of Soul Korea respectively, then try to explore those critical factors of creative culture districts in China. In order to identify the core successful factors to manage and market a creative culture districts in China, the cases study also analyzed the origination and implementation of the three cases with particular focus on the core successful factors for these creative culture districts.

The definition of creative culture districts is recognized as a city's well – recognized and labeled area with a high culture facilities' concentration for the anchor of attraction. Generally speaking, the creative culture districts are not only culture or art center where various of artists get together to engage in art activities, but also include many facilities such as office, retail, housing and art exchange center are mixed in the area, actually, these facilities formed a valuable chain affected each other. There are many cities in China are currently planning or have developed culture districts which are variously labeled culture arts sector, arts and entertainment district, arts and science district, and art districts, even more specialized labels such as theater district and museum district.

This dissertation will try to systematically identify and explore key factors to affect success of creative culture districts by using importance – performance measurement tool and stakeholder theory. Stakeholder refers to the different relative reference group to get involve or create same issues. It includes those structure, development and construction for the different affection of what these groups get involve in. This theory firstly has been used in managerial field for enterprise administration, it also in analyzing how to develop tourism management. The industrial cluster theory firstly use in studying these factors which relative to creative culture districts. This dissertation creatively conducted the theories into the study on creative culture districts in China on base of wildly literature review researching not only for various different stakeholders of Western countries' culture districts but also current situation of China' culture districts.

The study for culture districts in Western countries emerged in middle of 20 century, the phenomena can be explained by different fields such as economics, geography, new economy – geography, tourism science, social science etc. The hot points mainly focus on definition of culture districts, some issues about production and consuming structure, mechanism of culture district, measurement methods for culture district's performance and successful factors of culture district. In China, at the end of 20 century most of scholars mainly focus on conducting the concept, simply interpreting the phenomena of culture district, commentate for relationship of culture district and real estate, advocating the economic performance and identifying the successful and fail factors of culture district. Because lacking of relative theories support and deeply studying of western literature, most of these research could not reflect the real situation of culture districts.

The study integrates multiple knowledge and applies for stakeholder theories to analyze the cases, and try to explore the core successful factors of creative culture districts in China. The main purpose of using stakeholder theories is to find those major factors lead to success of culture districts by studying the internal and external components of stakeholder for cultural districts. On the other hand, important – performance method will be used as a tool to analyze those attributes that can greatly affect the culture districts' management and marketing activities. Finally, according to the theoretical and empirical analysis, this study suggested that one side, there are five critical factors for cultural district should be paid attention in China they are called strategic level factors include leadership and management of cultural district, no – profit organizations, the status of the community people, the government and the relevant departments and artist groups stakeholders. In order to make cultural district more successful, decision maker must consider above six factors and try to balance and deal with them as a general direction. One the other sides, through empirical research in 798 cultural district, the study found that the main purpose of tourists come to cultural district is just look around for its reputation and minority of them want to collect art works or develop exchange activities etc. Therefore, management and marketing plan should more concentrate on those factors related to service quality such as layout of the cultural district, enough parking places, clear signs for traffic, location of cultural district and quality of food

Abstract

provided etc.

Therefore, the study includes four chapters all together: The first chapter, the second chapter and the third chapter are introduction, literature review and analysis; the fourth chapter is findings and conclusions.

Content

Chapter One Introduction ·· 1
   1. Definition and Evolution of Creative Culture District ···················· 4
   2. Research Questions ··· 11
   3. Significance of the Study ··· 12
   4. Outline of Dissertation ··· 12

Chapter Two Literature Review ··· 13
   1. Cultural Districts: Notions and Issues ··· 13
   2. Review of Researcher Works ··· 18
   3. Researches in Domestic ··· 41
   4. Methodology ··· 51
   5. Three Successful Cases of Cultural District ······························ 56

Chapter Three Analysis of Cultural District in China ························· 72
   1. Importance—performance Analysis ··· 72
   2. Empirical Measurement for 798 Cultural District in
      China by Important - performance ·· 76
   3. Analysis for the Three Successful Cases ··································· 85

Chapter Four Findings and Conclusion ·· 96
   1. Findings ··· 96
   2. Conclusions ··· 102
   3. Policies and Recommendations ··· 104

Appendix A ·· 111
Appendix B ·· 113
References ·· 115

Chapter One Introduction

Communities' arts are a special group which was emerged after reform and open in China. They often get together in a specific area to develop art creative activities as professional practitioners and freelance artist, then this kind of getting together has become a painter village and art district. This phenomenon not only react something of free flow for globalization and market environment, but also some new changing of social evolutionary. Art district has become a major pattern of pursuing "Art Utopia" and this kind formation also became the earliest art community: "Painter Village." The real painter village in China emerged in twenty century 90th, the typical painter village is Yuan Ming Yuan painter village of BeiJing, but it has been finally forbidden by government in 1995. Although it was forbidden, the village became a beginning of development for art village in China. Certainly, the phenomenon of artists getting together has been existed early in Western country, from early Barbison School to "SOHO" art district of New York, the developing history as following:

Table 1 Development History of Art District New York

Name	Ages	Country	Remark
Barbison School	19 century $30-40^{th}$	France	Actually, Barbison School is not real meaning of nowadays art district, but it has some features of today's art districts. Barbison is the entrance of Paris Fontainebleau forest, some painters came here and settled down to develop art activities, increasingly form Barbison School
SOHO art district	20 century $50-60^{th}$	America New York	It is famous for creative culture district, it has became a commercial district and tourism area
Hell and art center	1976	America	Military base of US troops where located around San Francisco Golden Bridge, the troops moved out of there in 1976, the complex of building were abandoned. With artists moving in, it became a vitality area
Left bank art district		France	Senine River artists district

continued table

Name	Ages	Country	Remark
Dachau	19 century 1890 – 1914	Germany	Around Munich, swamp scenic spot of Ampere River, it attracts lots of artists because of beautiful scene
Worpswede art district	1889	Germany	Worpswede of Bremen, it was called "township of artists"
Eastern district of London	20 century 20th	England	At that time this area is poor section of town in London, with some young artists moving in, it became a famous art district in the world
Newcastle art district	20 century 90th	England	An art district in North of England, early it is a coal mining area abandoned, now it has become a unique art center

From the development of western countries' art district, with the transformation of industrial to post – industrial society, there are a lot of factory building and workshop were abandoned around city. It has attracted numbers of artists come here for settled down because of the huge space and low rental, finally formed vary kinds of art districts or painters village. Although it has different reasons for the formation, its nature is process of social & economic development and transformation.

In China, it emerged lots of cultural art district in short time such as early Yuanmingyuan painter village, Beijing 798 creative art district and Song Zhuang painter village. It also could be seen as an outcome of social development and cultural transformation. The major culture art district in China as following:

Table 2 The Major Cultural Art District in China

Name	Time	Location	Remark
Yuanmingyuan painter village	1990 – 1995	Beijing	Forbidden in 1995
Huajia land	1992 – 2004	Beijing	Vanish
Shanghai painter village	2001 – 2003	Shanghai	To attract painters by low rental, it was closed down because management
798 art district	2002 – today	Beijing	This district was appointed to be one of top ten in Beijing. As an center of artists village which include No. one art district, Caochang land art district etc

Chapter One Introduction

continued table

Name	Time	Location	Remark
Songzhuang artist village	1995 – today	Beijing Song village	Because yuanmingyuan village was vanished, one part of them moved to Songzhuang village to rent and brought house. It formed a famous artists district
Dafen village	1989 – today	Shenzhen	It is not a real painter village, in 1989 a business man came here to do sell paintings
Suzhou River	1998 – today	Shanghai	Many years ago there were lots of building located at the two sides of Suzhou River, recent years these building were abandoned, therefore it attracts lots of artists came because of low rental and huge space
Mogan Mountain art district (M50 art district)	2002 – today	Shanghai	Chunming woolen fabric manufactory abandoned 41000m² huge space for artists' activities
Creative Warehouse	1991 – today	Yunnan	An art community which was changed from abandoned factory
Dani painter village	2003 – today	Qingdao	It was established at Danigou village in 2003
Weihai painter village	2008 – today	Rongcheng	Projected 200000m², it includes workshop, training center and gallery
Fangzhi city art district	2007 – today	Xian	There are 35 workshop, 13000m² more than 60 artists
Niupeng art district	1997 – today	Hongkong	In 1997, business owner move out of the oil street and document warehouse, these houses were rented to more than twenty art groups at low price. Government found another factory for those art groups when the date expired

From above table we can see that there were many similar art districts, painter village and creative area in China since last century 90th besides the artist district in Beijing. These culture art districts have same point that most of them are located in those spaces where were abandoned such as 798 art district, Suzhou River art district and Niupeng art district etc, on the other hand, one of very important economic element which lead to these districts prosperous is low rental fees. Certainly, the artists keep their own core value to develop their art activities.

Obviously, these art developments has remained and been encouraged as a downtown activity has much to do with the perceived role of the arts in revitalizing declining central cities. Culture facilities, public art, and arts activities are being developed and organized in central cities with clearly stated developmental goals. Claims for arts development have included as following:

- The arts beautify, enliven, and animate an area.
- Arts facilities, activities, and their attendant support services such as administration and marketing provide employment.
- Cultural activities attract residents and tourists to the central city, and these visitors support adjacent businesses such as restaurants, lodging, retail and parking.
- The presence of the arts can raise property values, increase the profitability of surrounding businesses, and expand the tax base of a given area.
- The arts are cited as one of the quality – of – life issues considered in business relocation.
- The arts attract creative, well – educated employees.
- The arts contribute to the creativity and innovation of a community.

(Frost – Kumpf, 1998)

According to these attributes and supports for the success of creative cultural art district have motivated the decision maker to use them for the strategies of urban development across the China, therefore, if we can try to explore and identify those attributes that affect the cultural creative art district managed and ran successfully, we could make effective planning about marketing, management and strategies, it will make a great contribution for the strategies making for urban development by standing the view of management and operation. Certainly, it has different understanding and developing evolution for culture district between Western countries and China.

1. Definition and Evolution of Creative Culture District

In this section, we will introduce the different definition of culture district between Western countries and China, particularly, take America as an example to identify the definition. One specific strategy of arts development as a part of urban revitalization has been the creation of cultural districts (see Figure 1).

Chapter One Introduction

Figure 1 Directional Sign from 798 Culture Art District

Source: Photo by author (2015).

Generally, a cultural district① is defined as a well-recognized and labeled area of a city with a high concentration of cultural facilities②used as the anchor of attraction to the area. The area is generally geographically defined and other land uses (such as hospitality, retail, office, and housing) are mixed in this area. But the defining characteristic of cultural districts is the cultural facilities and activities that take place in this area. Currently, more and more cities in China have planned or developed cultural art districts as part of their revitalization strategies within the last ten years. A wide range of land uses and landscapes reasonably can be labeled culture districts, and they also occupy a range of geographic locations within downtown or occasionally at their

---

① Culture district here, actually it is the dissertation topic mentioned "creative culture art district", although the causing formed is different, they have the same characteristics and functions, therefore, in this paper the term used "culture district".

② Culture facilities are defined here as the specialized spaces designed to serve the production and presentation of arts, historic, or humanities activities, such as museums, concert halls, theaters, art galleries artists' studios, rehearsal halls, as well as the administrative support services that directly serve these kinds of activities.

fringe[①]. Many cities have specific areas that might be recognized cultural based upon public perceptions of a high concentration of theaters, museums, or galleries. But most such areas are not formally designated as cultural. However, some urban areas are designated by terms such as cultural district or arts district by a number of institutions within the city, including government agencies, private development groups, promotional bureaus, or some organizations special in dealing with selling arts products. This label ranges in formality from a legal designation in a zoning ordinance to simply consistent use over time in a variety of planning and promotional documents.

Culture districts are specialized landscapes that offer participation in and consumption of cultural activities. The facilities considered by planners of cultural districts to be cultural generally appear to be spaces supporting the fine arts such as concert halls, theaters, galleries, and art museums as well as libraries, historical museums, and educational institutions. The activities in cultural districts are usually "high" culture or "fine arts", although the meaning of culture appears to vary among cultural districts. Some districts labeled as cultural contain such things as restaurants, nightclubs, and more popular entertainment. Social theorist Raymond Williams traces the historical roots and development of the word culture and provides three definitions that he sees in contemporary usage in his book keywords (Willianms, 1985):

(1) Culture as the general process of intellectual, spiritual and aesthetic development;

(2) Culture as a particular way of life, whether of a people, a period, a group, or humanity in general;

(3) Culture as the works and practices of intellectual and especially artistic activity.

His third definition of culture appears to be a more common understanding. A survey by Louis Harris and associates in 1973 for Americans, "what does the word culture mean to you?" The primary responses were:

---

① This kind of fringes often is abandoned factories, and lots of artists get together here because of the low rental fees and huge spaces.

Chapter One Introduction

Table 3 Response for Definition of Culture

Responses	Percentage (%)
the arts (music, theatre, dance, visual arts, museums, historical sites, etc.)	37
Education and learning	19
Lifestyle, way people live, behavior	16
Refinement, finer things, anything uplifting	14
Historical background of people: Customs and traditions	12

Source: Associated Councils for the arts, 1975.

Furthermore, culture, as popularly understood, often appears to imply a distinction between "fine" or "high" art and "popular" arts and entertainment (Gans, 1974). DiMaggio (1982) and Levine (1988) have documented the history of organizations in the United States purposely segmenting themselves and their products as high culture and popular culture, defining the cannon of "serious" works of culture as distinct from mere entertainment (DiMaggio, 1991). While the American Assembly's study showed questions about Americans' mixed perceptions of "popular culture" and "high culture".

Indeed, when asked about the definition of culture being used in the cultural districts, all of the district representatives interviewed seemed surprised at the question, perhaps as if the meaning was self-evident. According to their suggested that "culture as arts and intellect" seemed to be what they intended. Most of the cultural districts observed tend to have a concentration of arts facilities, libraries or museums and to reflect the high-status, fine or non-commercial art forms, occasionally, some entertainments spaces (e.g. movie theaters, nightclubs, and other spaces providing commercial art forms) could be also included in these districts.

In addition to containing culture facilities, culture districts are mixed-use developments that contain such non-culture land uses as office complexes, convention spaces, hospitality facilities, retail spaces, and occasionally residential areas. Many culture districts have been created in or near central business districts and are often contiguous to newly developed corporate office complexes. They sometimes are developed near or contain elements of what sociologist Patrick Mullins (1991) has labeled "consumption compounds". These consumption compounds may include tourism and convention centers, gentrified housing for up-scale residents, restored historic buildings and heritage districts, and reclaimed industrial sites and waterfronts transformed into festival retail markets. In fact, the involvement of cultural facilities in

基于重要性和表现维度的中国创意文化产业区分析

the re-development of city spaces is not a new phenomenon. Labeled cultural spaces were created in United States cities beginning in the late 19 century and through the 1930s during earlier periods of urban change (Peterson, 1976; Steffensen - Bruce, 1998; Wilson, 1989). Cultural facilities of may kinds were proposed and developed during the City Beautiful movement (approximately 1893 - 1909) and later during the Depression in the 1930s. New museums, auditoriums, aquariums, and libraries were built, motivate in part by the desire for city beautification, economic development, and the perceived "civilizing" influence of an aesthetic urban environment (Wilson, 1989). The result was a considerable number of culturally - focused urban spaces or "cultural compounds" (Frost - Kumpf, 1998). These early cultural compounds do not quite fit the definition of cultural district used in this study. The cultural attractions in these compounds were primarily major museums, large performing halls, theaters, or auditoriums, and sometimes schools, colleges, libraries, planetariums or zoos. In these early cultural compounds, the non - cultural land uses (the mixed - use aspect of the district) tended to be limited to parks, arboreta, hospitals or housing. Very few of those early cultural districts included commercial uses such as office complexes, hospitality facilities and retail spaces. This is the main features of early cultural districts. We can give some examples for the early cultural districts in America, during the early twentieth century of Chicago's central business district, the development in Chicago of the Art Institute, Orchestra Hall, the Field Museum, and the Shedd Aquarium all date to the period of massive re - development. It includes the infill of considerable acreage of lakefront property to accommodate theses new cultural facilities. This kind area, which has been called a "cultural campus," has been an important part of the city's identity and a tourist attraction to Chicago's inner loop area (Furnweger, 1999).

Cultural compounds were often constructed like university campuses, with fairly large open green spaces among the buildings. Some of these districts were originally built in areas some what removed from their cities' central business districts. Like these kinds of districts, however, were built in an earlier era of city growth. While their location at the time of construction may have been at the edge of the city, these cities have since grown considerably beyond their older boundaries. Thus, these districts appear, from a modern perspective, to be located in the central city.

For example, in Fort Worth, a cultural compound was created on the city's west side during the Depression as one of many facilities created across the United States by the federally funded Works Progress Administration. The Fort Worth Zoo and the Will

Chapter One Introduction

Rogers Memorial Coliseum were created during the 1930s and later supplemented by the Casa Mnana Theatre, the Kimball Museum, and the Amon Carter Museum during the 1950s. Other examples of earlier cultural compound development in the United States are Cleveland's University Circle, Dallas' Fair Park, and St. Louis' Forest Park. Cultural compounds continue to be important elements in many cities' economic and cultural growth, and their facilities continue to be remodeled or expanded and sometimes included in modern cultural districts, actually, so called modern cultural districts also include creative cultural districts.

However, many of the modern cultural districts also appear to have been developed in response to problems connected with arts complexes built in major American cities during the 1950s and 1960s. Two examples of such facilities include the Kennedy Center in Washington, DC and the Performing Arts Center of Los Angeles County. Some critics had complained that these arts facilities were both physically and programmatically isolated from their surrounding neighborhoods (Berelowitz, 1993; Kaplan, 1989; Kay, 1983). Architectural elements of these structures—walls, parking lots, and entrance ways these were seen as barriers designed to protect those who attend arts activities from the surrounding, often economically depressed, central city neighborhoods. Programming in such centers has been criticized for ignoring the needs of local residents. Obviously, cultural district has covered an evolution process in America, the old cultural district can be associated with the modern era of central city redevelopment in the United States. Such districts may have elements of earlier cultural facilities (or even earlier cultural compounds) such as old concert halls, movie theaters, or Carnegie libraries, but these facilities usually have been considerably remodeled or converted to new uses. These new cultural districts have large concentration of new development and are considerably more mixed – use than the earlier cultural compounds.

In China, cultural district emerged not so long time, it hasn't been researched deeply by scholars because of the forbidden of early painters village disputes. With recent years' rapid development of cultural district and it is valued by government, at mean while, some cultural districts has generated a great influence in the world, therefore, the special phenomenon causes attention and develop great scale research and discussion. It also has conducted great researching contributions, some of them are really have great value.

To summarize these researches, most of them around Beijing cultural districts particularly, 798 cultural district is typical example for the development of cultural district in China. In this study, we mainly use the example as our research case to identify the historical evolution, structure, mechanism and problems for development of cultural district in China.

Firstly, those materials that come from artists, organizations and district management office provided rich history lecture materials. The materials include *Beijing* 798: *The Recreated "Factory"*, it introduced two stages of factory and cultural district by word and pictures. It has showed us clearly 798 cultural districts past and present situations. *Beijing* 798was edited by Chenglei and Zhuqi. It not only discussed the problems and contradiction through about twenty artists and experts who got involved to construct 798 cultural district, but also explored and identify current situation and developing difficulties on new vision. Although this book analyzed the develop strategy and difficult position for 798 cultural district, it didn't present the interaction relationship of inner multi-element in cultural district. On the other hand, it ignored the interest transfer of different stake holders in commercial surrounding and cultural district construction and deconstruction.

Secondly, research for 798 cultural district and Songzhuang painter village. During 2003 and 2005, scholars developed great deal of research for the districts because 798 cultural district was going to be removed by government, it caused great attention by lots of people. Fang lili developed a research for the district "Research Report for 798 Cultural District". This report includes four parts: Evolution, formation and analysis, interview and 798 cultural district's future. At that time, three meetings were also opened respectively like forum which was participated by art practitioners in 798 cultural district, mainly discussed future developing strategies and a conversation meeting which was attended by decision maker from government. The writer made social questionnaire, comparison and statistic analysis report for 798 cultural districts. On the other sides, it made two research reports respectively for "Beijing International Art Campus" and Songzhuang town painter village; it is regarded as a completed report for these cultural districts. However, because the time of bringing about this report is to provide a decision making evidence for government to decide whether remove 798 cultural district or not with a intentionality, therefore, this report only focus on the great value of district. Some issues haven't been got involved into this report such as cultural ecology, interactive relationship between different level internal of 798 cultural district and future developing strategies, particularly, those issues of cultural transformation, economic changing and forming mechanism haven't been touched deeply.

Thirdly, Wang weijiain 2005 has developed research for the strategies of 798 cultural district through sending questionnaire to interview visitors from all over the world. Finally, he conduced valuable strategies and programs for development of 798 cultural district. Yu changjiang in 2006 published "Songzhuang: The Art Community Under Globalization Background" in *Art Review* to described and analyzed artists group in Songzhuang painter village through concept of "edge", it shows that avant – garde neither live in the center of city nor in the village because of living cost and the heresy features. It is under this situation that artists hard to find a place for long term settling down.

Fourthly, some academic degree dissertation papers focus on cultural district. Those papers discussed issues related to cultural district such as art market, art & cultural industrial, art creation and artists' life etc. Art market and art cultural industrial have been cause people's great attention through checking all of those papers. One problem here is that those papers hardly seen the cultural & art issues as a whole but reflected only one side of them.

Summarizing above researches, the researching for cultural & art district seldom focus on the issues about management of cultural districts', developing strategy and marketing. Probably, research of cultural district and cultural district knowledge were conducted into business school not so long time. It ignores how to guarantee the cultural district develop successfully by making right marketing strategies and managerial methods.

2. Research Questions

The study was mainly designed to address two research questions concerning cultural district: ①What factors are the core elements for influencing cultural district develop successfully? ②How can we make effective marketing strategy and decision to guarantee a success marketing plan? It is obvious that this study of cultural districts in China is an exploratory investigation of an understudies phenomenon. Currently, there are not so many researches for cultural district by combining managerial issues to the operation of cultural district in China. Because most of cultural districts in China were build by local government, which always ignore considering those issues about marketing, customer needs, and marketing strategies etc or they have comparative weak capability of making marketing management to lead to the failure of operating the cultural district. However, each of local government has proposed cultural district and appear to be relying on these strategies to revitalize local area and their economy. Therefore, this study will produce detailed findings about the phenomenon that can be used to ground future research on the success of failure of such strategies.

3. Significance of the study

Cultural districts are a growing phenomenon in China. Every year, more local government indicate an interest in the use of this strategy to revitalize the economy and improve tourism industrial, even a degraded section of downtown, or a problematic neighborhood. A huge money are being invested in communities across the country in the planning and development of cultural district in China. Base on the goal statements published by the planners of cultural districts, these developments are expected to have a significant impact on reversing urban decay by attracting new visitors, increasing investment in the area, and assisting cities in restoring lost tax revenue and land value. An important aspect of successful operating a cultural district depends on making a mix of effective and feasible marketing, management plan. Therefore, these issues must be well understood, and the management strategies must be carefully described and analyzed.

4. Outline of Dissertation

Chapter One is a discussion of the problem statement, definition and evolution of cultural district, significant of this study. In Chapter Two, it is about literature review and methodology include western country's cultural district development, particular America is taken example and some contributions were achieved by researchers in China. Chapter Three is case comparison analysis. Chapter Four is empirical analysis of the core successful factors. Findings and conclusions is included in Chapter Five.

Chapter Two   Literature Review

1. Cultural Districts: Notions and Issues

In the scientific literature, the term of a "Cultural District" has been used in different ways by a number of authors in a variety of research field (Frosk – Kumpf, 1998; Hitters & Richards, 2002; Lazzeretti, 2003; Santagata, 2002; Stern & Seifert, 1998; Zukin, 1995). As a consequence, the term has not yet acquired an unequivocal definition. One major stream of research (Frost – Kumpf, 1998; Seifert & Stern, 2005; Stern & Seifert, 1998; Zukin, 1995) examines cultural districts within the context of urban planning policies. For example, defines cultural district as "a well – recognized, labeled, mixed – use area of a city in which a high concentration of cultural facilities serves as the anchor of attraction" (Frost – Kumpf, 1998). According to this view, cultural districts also called "cultural cluster" are tools in the hands of urban planning authorities for fostering the development of urban centers and revitalizing neighborhoods in decline. The underlying insight here is that, as urban economies grow increasingly reliant not just on the production of culture, but also on its consumption, culture acquires the potential to become a powerful driver of local development. However these benefits of cultural districts come at a cost. Critics of cultural districts point out that one negative consequence of this type of planning is that it legitimizes the separation of rich areas from other areas, thereby contributing to create markers of social and cultural distinction within the city (Zukin, 1995). There is therefore a risk that cultural districts may drive out, or "displace", lower income long – time residents due to rises in real – estate and living costs (Stern & Seifert, 1998). Other authors in the same field (Stern & Seifert, 1998) adopt a model of cultural district that places less emphasis on externally driven and coordinated development, introducing the concept of "natural" rather than imposed – cultural districts. Natural cultural districts are envisaged as spatially delimited areas in which a varied array of cultural assets are clustered, but whose evolution occurs "organically as a result of individual agents creators and participants, producers and consumers – deciding to locate themselves near one another" (Seifert & Stern, 2005).

In contrast, a somewhat broader conceptualization of cultural districts is that proposed by the work of the international center for Research on the Economics of Culture, Institution and Creativity (University of Turin, Italy). For example, Santagata (2002) describes cultural districts as "geographically clustered networks of interdependent entities defined by the production of idiosyncratic goods based on creativity and intellectual property". This author identifies four types of cultural districts: Industrial cultural districts, institutional cultural districts, museum cultural districts and metropolitan cultural districts – with this last type being very similar to the cultural districts envisaged in the stream of literature on urban planning policy. Further, Ghafele and Santagata (2006) employ the concept of "Tourist Cultural District", "mighty conglomeration of natural, historical and social resources" in which "ameities and cultural experiences are integrated into the tourist space". According to these authors, two conditions are required for such districts to develop. First, the agents participating in the production of the "tourism product" must be clustered within a limited geographical area permeated with natural beauty and culture. Second, the cultural factor, which also contributes in large part to the "tourism product", must be idiosyncratic to the local community. A further analysis of the idea of cultural districts can be found in the work of Sacco, Tavano Blessi, and Nuccio (2008). These Authors argue that a distinctive trait of culture is its ability to promote a system – wide integration of diversified activities, and that this integration occurs both within a single value chain (vertical integration) and across value chains (horizontal integration). Accordingly, the authors put forward the definition of "system – wide cultural district" as "an idiosyncratic mix of top – down planned elements and emergent, self – organised activities coalescing into a model of local development in which cultural activity displays significant strategic complementarities with other production chains within typical post – industrial contexts" (Sacco, Tavano Blessi & Nuccio, 2008). Though they take differing perspectives, all the above contributions agree on one fundamental point: That cultural district are conducive to endogenous and sustainable growth and may successfully revitalize depressed areas (Evans, 2001; Frost – Kumpf, 1998; Hitters & Richards, 2002; Lazzeretti, 2003; Sacco, Tavano Blessi & Nuccio, 2008; Santagata,

Chapter Two Literature Review

2002). However this revitalization and growth should not be characterized solely in terms of sustainability, because sustainability alone, as argued in Ryan (2002), "is insufficient as an objective". Instead, Ryan proposes a wider view represented by the concept of "sustained value creation", according to which tourism industry managers should strive to provide added value to environments, entrepreneurs and tourists. This is also the perspective which we endorse in this work.

Drawing on the contributions outlined above, a working definition of the term cultural district was formulated for this study. Based in particular on the notions of system – wide (Sacco, Tavano Blessi & Nuccio, 2008) and "Tourist Cultural Districts" (Ghafele & Santagata, 2006), and complemented by the concept of sustained value creation described in Ryan (2002), a cultural district is envisaged as a system of interdependent entities—including public and private institutions, businesses, entrepreneurs, individuals and local communities—situated within a limited geographical area, aimed at achieving sustained value creation, and driven by the unifying role of culture. Cultural district evolve from a mixture of top – down planned and emergent activities involving a large set of stakeholders belonging to different value chains. Within such a context, local culture and traditions are fundamental ingredients of the cultural and tourism products of a district.

A cultural district, defined above, is characterized by interconnections between multiple systems (value chains) and a large number of stakeholders, who represent diverse and sometimes conflicting interests. Given this level of intricacy, a cultural district may be described as "complex" (Trist, 1983) or, according to Farrell and Twining – Ward (2004), as a "complex adaptive system" that requires attention to spatial and temporal factors, and to decision making dynamics. Conceptualizing complex systems such as cultural districts is thus an inherently challenging activity, and several issues can potentially threaten this ambitious endeavor. To identify what these issues are, we have drawn from the literature on collaborative planning processes and stakeholder collaboration, with specific reference to the tourism context. The literature on tourism planning projects is relevant to our analysis because these interventions resemble cultural district projects on at least three levels. First, a tourism system is a "complex planning domain" (Jamal & Stronza, 2009), and thus shares this distinctive trait with cultural districts. Second, a cultural district, as envisaged in this study, is in itself a tourism destination (Ghafele & Santagata, 2006), though one in which the cultural dimension plays a prominent role. And third, several studies support the use of tourism as a tool for the revitalization and long-term development of local communities (Besculides, Lee & McCormick, 2002; Joppe, 1996; Silberberg, 1995), which is another distinctive trait of cultural districts. Following the seminal paper of Jamal and Getz (1995), a number of authors have widely explored collaboration theory in tourism management, examining a range of related questions from different perspectives. From the investigations into how cultural districts can be constructed and used to foster long-term development, three main issues emerge as relevant: *The initial identification and involvement of key stakeholders; the maintenance of the collaboration process; and the (long-term) implementation of collaborative outcomes.*

Firstly, *the identification and involvement of key stakeholders* during the early stages of collaboration was already identified as pivotal in the seminal contributions on collaboration theory (Gray, 1985, 1989; Gray & Hay, 1986). This issue has remained of great importance in several subsequent studies (Aas et al., 2005; Bramwell & Sharman, 1999; Gray, 1989; Hayward, 1988; Jamal & Getz, 1995; Ritchie, 1993; Sheehan & Ritchie, 2005; Vernon et al., 2005), in which it has been further explored and specified. For example Jamal and Getz (1995) note that selection of stakeholders is closely bound up with two other important aspects of collaborative processes: Legitimacy and power. These authors interpret legitimacy, with reference to Gray (1985), as both the right and capacity of a given stakeholder to be involved in a collaboration, arguing that a legitimate stakeholder "must also have the resources and skills (capacity) needed to participate" (Jamal & Getz, 1995). The power aspect is discussed, directly or indirectly, in various other contributions. Some authors (Hall, 1999; Tosun, 1998, 2000) focus on the weaker voices, clearly recognizing the difficulties which less powerful stakeholders face as a result of unbalanced power distributions. Stoker (1995), meanwhile, argues that the formation of powerful coalitions, where stakeholders seek to collaborate only with those who share compatible goals and resources while ignoring or marginalizing others, may threaten the success of collaboration.

Secondly, the distribution of power within a collaborative arrangement ties in with the second of the previously identified main issues, namely *the maintenance of a collaboration process*. This topic area has been progressively explored in the literature, identifying a number of elements which play a part. The first element, found to be significant in early studies (Gray & Hay, 1986; Ritchie, 1988), is consensus-based decision making. Its importance has been widely recognized in the tourism literature

(Aas et al., 2005; Bramwell & Sharman, 1999; Jamal & Getz, 1995; Vernon et al., 2005), indicating broad agreement that a collaboration process lacking consensus may strongly impede attainment of both short and long term objectives. A second element, related to consensus, is the role of information sharing. In this connection, scholars have outlined the importance of widespread and shared access to information (Gray, 1989) and mutual consultation, and information dissemination (Bramwell & Sharman, 1999). A further element which emerges as important in exploring the maintenance of large collaborations is heterogeneity (Jamal & Stronza, 2009; Medeiros de Araujo & Bramwell, 2002; Sheehan & Ritchie, 2005). In their study, Edward, Goodwin, Pemberton, and Woods (2000) define heterogeneity within collaborations in term of diversity of governance structures, including focuses, scales of operation, duration and histories, patterns of sector representation and funding. Ritchie (1993) instead defines heterogeneity in terms of different value systems brought to the collaboration process by each stakeholder. Finally, the tourism literature has also highlighted the evolution of roles as an important element for maintenance of collaborations. Notable examples of this are the temporal factor referred to in Farrell and Twining – Ward (2004) and Jamal and Stronza (2009), or the changing roles of actors mentioned by Vernon et al. (2005).

Thirdly, the main identified issue is the (long – term) implementation of collaborative outcomes. Despite the arguable importance of this topic, it has received only little attention in the tourism literature. Two notable exceptions are the studies of Bramwell and Sharman (1999) and Jamal and Stronza (2009). In their research, Bramwell and Sharman assert that the "extent to which stakeholders accept that there are systemic constraints on what is feasible" (Bramwell & Sharman, 1999) is important for avoiding unrealistic expectations of the collaboration process implementation. Jamal and Stronza (2009), on the other hand, specifically analyze two aspects relating to the challenges of long term implementation of collaborative outcomes, namely long term structuring, and outcomes of collaborations involving local communities and residents. On the other hand, the collaboration and tourism literature has identified a number of issues which play a relevant role in collaborative processes. Out of these, the study consider those which can potentially arise during the conceptualization phase of a collaborative project, such as empirical setting, and which may also have an impact in subsequent phases of the project. The issues identified are shown in Table 4.

Table 4 Those Potential Issues in Cultural District

Area	Issues
Identification and involvement of key stakeholders maintaining the collaboration	Involvement in the collaboration Representation: Legitimacy and power capacity to participate Power distribution among the convened stakeholder Need for consensus – based decision making
Long term implementation of the collaborative outcomes	Information sharing and dissemination Heterogeneity in governance structures and value systems Evolution of the roles of actors Long term outcomes and structuring of the collaboration process Unrealistic expectations

2. Review of Researcher Works

Cultural district has been studied by many researchers through lots of tools and theories and standing many views for analysis. Michela Arnabldi, Nicola Spiller (2011) take the case of cultural district as an example by using of Actor – network theory to explore the mechanism of cultural district operation. The research topic investigated was the conceptualization of a cultural district. Using the working definition given previously, it implied conceptualizing a system of interdependent entities situated within a limited geographical area, aimed at achieving sustained value creation driven by the unifying role of culture. To tackle the complexity of this relational setting, Actor – Network (ANT) was adopted as a framework. Actor – Network (ANT) is a socio – philosophical approach which attempts to comprehend complex social situations by paying attention to relational elements. The reason why many researchers would like to use this method is the increasing popularity of ANT arises from a pivotal, though feature: The symmetrical treatment of human and no – human actors, and of social and technical elements (Latour, 1996, 2005; Law, 1992). Under ANT, these heterogeneous elements are attributed equal importance and are seen as part of dynamic and never definitive networks, in which the essence for understanding sociological phenomena lies in the associations among them. However, it also has been put forward as an innovative research approach in tourism studies (Van der Duim, 2007; van der Duim & van Marwijk, 2006). The three elements of ANT for tourism management are principle of symmetry, the focus on actor-works, and the emphasis on processes of translation. The second feature of interest is at the core of how ANT conceptualizes social spaces. Viewed in this light, actors both human and non-human form and participate in networks, so it is only by following these actors (Latour, 1987, 1996, 2005) and their associations that social and scientific phenomena can be understood. The third element identified by van der Duim (2007) is translation (Latour, 1987) arguably the most endorsed feature of ANT in innovation studies (McLean & Hassard, 2004). According to ANT, innovation and its conceptualization should not be viewed as rationally predictable achievements, but rather as a fluid and erratic translation. In accordance with the ANT perspective, the author treats the conceptualization of a cultural district not as a rational, predetermined path to be followed, but rather as a process of translation. The cultural district is an innovation that needs to be promoted, developed and shaped by creating associations between individuals, objects and information (Van der Duim, 2007). Although Latour (1987) cautions against conceiving of this translation as a rational, predictable path, he sets out a number of rules for scientists seeking to promote their innovations. The analysis of the issues involved in building a cultural district led to an initial framework based upon three rules: Enrolling actors, fact building and circulating translations. Firstly, the author suggests that *enrolling actors* was empirically found to be crucial from the outset of the conceptualization. Among the related issues identified in the initial framework. The first seminal activation condition proved to be the need to garner sufficient involvement and collect ideas about the cultural district, further enrolments were then not triggered according to any pre-established plan, but rather in response to other activation conditions, for resolving controversies or re-orienting the process towards sustained value creation (Ryan, 2002); the second activation condition was the emergence of dysfunctional collaboration due to imbalances in power distribution among actors, a situation marked by failure to consider certain dimensions of long-term sustainability; the third activation condition was tied to certain stakeholders lacking adequate competencies pertaining to the project, this was especially critical for the partner organizations that needed to build the necessary competencies, also with a view to the future management of the district. Secondly, this study believed that *fact – building* was one of ANT element used. In Latour's Machiavellian perspective (Chua, 1995; Gendron et al., 2007) fact – building is central to helping persuade people, deal with controversies and divert interests (Latour, 1987, 2005). The study findings here confirmed the importance of fact – building in relation to the outlined issues, and the empirical data also yielded some general conditions under which this rule is beneficial. Fact – building was applied to illustrate the cultural idea according to the framework. Given the multidisciplinary and intangible nature of these types of projects, it is unlikely that all the stakeholders initially enrolled possess the competencies to understand their holistic and complex nature, as well as the full range of opportunities and risks. The process of fact – building also can avoid generating overly high expectations about financial flows, it was used here to mitigate enthusiasm by simulating investment scenarios and the attendant resource commitments. However, there are two issues clearly emerged from the diagram: First, the prospected interventions exceeded the financial resources available overall. Second, the management costs, upon release of the project, would be sustained directly by the local actors participating in the cultural district. Thirdly, it is *circulating translations*. The study think that one of the characteristics of the conceptualization phase, especially in complex cultural projects, is its dynamic and fluid nature: Circulating inscriptions (Latour, 1987) about the district's evolution was crucial to keeping the partners and other actors committed to the project. Circulation is often associated with fact – building, but is itself also activated under certain conditions. The activation condition included in the framework referred to insufficient involvement of stakeholder in the conceptualization. The study suggests that in response to this, various strategies were enacted to circulate translations and regain a balanced involvement: A plenary presentation, an extensive survey (providing and collecting information), individual meetings, and focus groups. All these devices helped to disseminate the concept of the district across the local community, enlarging the panel of stakeholders that interacted with the core group of partners. Finally, the author formed a diagram to illustrate conditional path for the conceptualization of a cultural district project as follow:

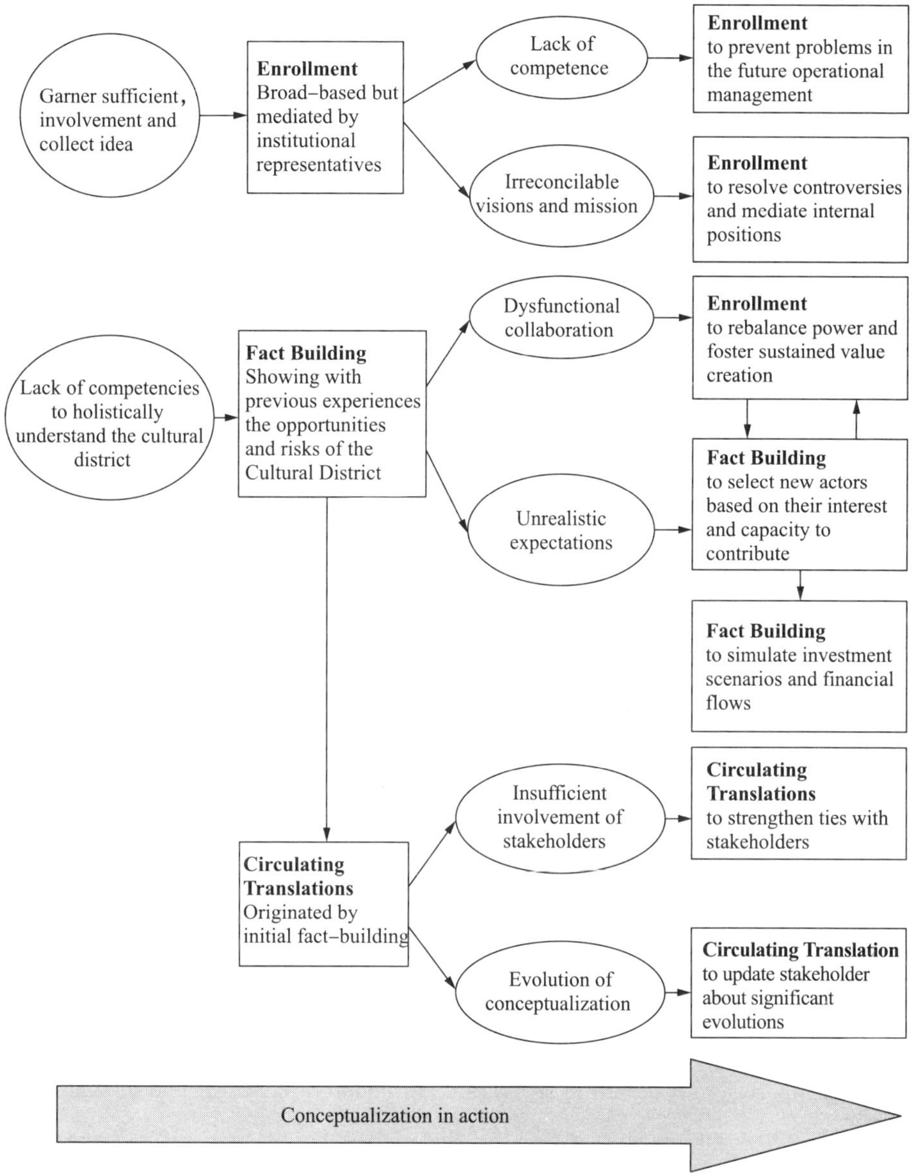

Chapter Two Literature Review

Diagram 1 Conditional Path of the Conceptualization of a Cultural Project

From above approach, it described in this study offers a novel perspective for the management of cultural district. Given that a rigid sequential definition of steps seems to be inappropriate, the author suggest here that a conditional path may be a viable alternative to complete lack of planning or just general indications. The project under this study also showed that there are recurrent causes of problems which can be tackled by specific actions, resulting in quicker reactions in seizing opportunities and facing difficulties. Actually, this study tries to analyze the relationship elements of actor – network and stakeholder collaboration rather than the cultural district itself, but author has made an approach and tool which can bring about an operation mechanism for researching cultural districts.

Se Hoon Park (2015) try to broaden knowledge on policy governance of cultural districts, particularly those utilizing artist communities for urban revitalization. The author believed that with the rise of the cultural economy in post – industrial cities in South Korea, cultural strategies have become key components in almost every urban regeneration project. Author found that over the past few years these strategies have fail to meet expectations and have often resulted in conflicts between artists and the government, in order to understand the factors behind the strategies' positive and negative consequences, this study examined three projects with different degrees of government intervention: ①The Totagoga Project in Busan City; ②The Daein Art Market project in Gwangju City; ③The Changdong Art Village project in Changwon City. This research mainly focuses on the mode of government intervention in the relationships among the government, artists, intermediary agencies, and local citizens. By putting the mode of government intervention in the context of social relations of related players in the cultural districts, it also tries to understand how similar policy schemes created different consequences. Base on the previous research, the study tries to further develop a discourse on effective governance in planning cultural districts, and cultural strategies in general, in the context of policy delivery practices in Korea. Research focuses are placed on the three points: Social – political relations among actors, the meaning of culture represented by the projects and changes in the mode of government interventions toward local issues, particularly under the "developmentalist" tradition in Korea and broadly in East Asia. Firstly, this study tries to locate the discourse on planning cultural districts in the frame of social – political relations among players in cultural districts, such as the national government, local urban bureaucrats, artists, merchants and citizens. The political aspects of culture – led urban regenerations have become a frequent focus of academic discussions in recent years (Grodach & Silver, 2012; Lin & Hsing, 2009; Shin & Stevens, 2013). The author raised up two questions that hasn't been caused enough attention is how different actors with different interests actually collaborate and /or come into conflict with each other in the development of cultural districts, and how these relations produce different results. Secondly, the author focus on how culture was interpreted and represented by each project, often as a compromise involving the different strategies of actors in developing cultural districts. It is that to say that urban bureaucrats, artists and local merchants usually have different understandings of culture, which make it hard for them to come together for consensus goals. Thirdly, the study tries to widen the knowledge on the changing modes of government intervention and its limitations in terms of local issues in South Korea, however the traditional mode of government intervention has been challenged and transformed, with more active participation from local civil actors. In this regard, this paper tries to discern the diverse experiments in the modes of government intervention in engaging local matters, particularly in cultural district planning in Korea.

The Changdong Art Village is one of the urban regeneration projects in Changdong, Changwon City, in South Kyeongsang Province. Since the 1990s, the area has failed to attract customers and visitors due to the suburban relocation of administrative functions and businesses and manufacturing industries in the city. Since 2006, the Changdng area was selected by the Ministry of Land, Transport and Maritime Affairs (MLTM) to conducted into a large - scale research project on development practices focused on physical development as a part of a "test bed" of national urban regeneration strategies with high attention and with a huge city government fund. Certainly, it is significant for both the national government and local government initiated project was successful, but there is one problem emerged that is the urban regeneration division of the city government had long deal with physical redevelopment projects, had no experience in cooperating with artists. The behaviors of government officials are tried to control artists "office hours" to enhance the image of an art district where people can look at the artists in their shops. The government also wanted to control the art studios' signboard designs, disregarding artists' individual tastes, to give the district a fancy and standardized aesthetic. Although most artists were attracted to the district on an individual basis with emotional attachments, what they wanted most were affordable work spaces and a stable work environment rather than revitalization of the district, on the other side, local merchants' prominent interest was placed on their own business rather than on promoting culture and reimaging the area. With increasing of visitor numbers in the district, merchants were divided into several different groups which interpreted the project differently by the actors: As a tool for pursuing the public goal of urban regeneration for urban bureaucrats, as an opportunity to secure affordable working spaces for artists, and as an instrument to spur other business opportunities for local merchants. Because of no clear leadership to coordinate the different interests and bring cooperation, the project soon faltered and conflicts between the government and artists began to emerge. The government tried to set up another steering committee to replace the commissioned management body and to gain full control of the project, the government also is looking for a new agency to operate the project. Finally, the government successfully operates the cultural district and won a prize from the Ministry of Land, Infrastructure and Transport as a model of cultural – led urban regeneration in Korea.

Daein Art Market in Gwangju is a traditional marketplace that developed as people gathered around vacant spaces near the Kwangju Railway Station shortly after the Korean War broke out in 1950. The area started to lose its population and customers in the early 1990s. A group of artists began occupying some of the vacant shops in the market when the artists funded by the Gwangju city government launched the market revitalization project as a side event of the Gwangju Biennale in 2008. Unlike the Changdng Art Village project, which focused on providing workspace to artists, the Daein Art Market project tries to assist artists and merchants only in an indirect way, with a view toward transforming the declining market into a cultural space for citizens. There is a so called "art market" where artists and merchants can coexist in harmony. The project team rents several shops in the market and operates them for the benefit of both artists and merchants. Among other services, the team provides galleries for artists and citizens, arranges education programs for merchants and citizens, and organizes annual festivals and a night art market for citizens (Daein Art Market Project Nuetinamusup, 2011). In this project, the role of the government is limited and marginal. The project is mostly run by the commissioned operating body, which is composed of local cultural planners and activists. It is obvious that the project team tries to function as a partner to both artists and merchants.

Totatoga art cluster in Busan, Totagoga is the name of the project implemented in the old downtown area of Busan, the second largest city in Korea. In the early 1990s, the area started to lose businesses and population after the city expanded into surrounding areas with new land developments. Under the project, the city government provides a group of selected artists with workspace by making use of vacant offices through an operating agency in the district for a three year period. In return, artists are required to engage in local activities, such as running education programs and holding

Figure 2　Daein Art Market

cultural festivals for local citizens. The artists receive three years of government support and then are encouraged to be self – supporting in their spaces. If the project is successful, more and more artists will be attracted to central Busan. The uniqueness of the project lies not only in the idea of how to incorporate artists into urban revitalization, but also in the way in which the project is implemented and operated. In operating the project, the city government was sidelined, and the cultural planners and artists played key roles. The commissioned management body had a strong network with local artists in Busan and liaised expertly with city officials, artists and citizens. They persuaded building owners in the old downtown to rent their vacant spaces at 15% below market price and worked closely with the committed and motivated artists. However, they were not just mediating agents allocating funds to artists, but also facilitators and moderators ensuring that everything worked harmoniously. This leadership has stimulated other artists' volunteer spirit and has spurred their engagement in local communities. Ironically, the rather apathetic attitude of the city government contributed significantly to the natural blossoming of the cultural cluster in the district. Due to the leeway created by this non – interventionist mode of operation, the artists were more motivated to plan their actions and engage in communities in the district. The leadership of cultural planners and local artists played a pivotal role in creating a difference in the district. Although the attitude of the city government has now changed from uninterested to attentive and supportive, the artists in the cultural district now hope that this government attention will lead to more support rather than excessive control.

In this study, the author presented three different modes of government intervention for controlling the project procedure. In the case of Changdong, the local government aggressively pushed the project and tried to control the whole implementation process. Under the government's tight control, the cultural planners and the selected artists had no room to release their creative talents for the community. On the other hand, in the case of Daein Art Market, the city government tried to be a "partner" rather than a director. The government intended to achieve its policy goals by taking advantage of a number of artists already settled in the market. In the Togatoga project, because of the strong initiative of local cultural activists and committed artists, the role of the government was limited to providing funds behind the scenes on the manner of a "patron". Standing on the view of operation mode, in the government – led cultural district projects, culture was often translated by urban bureaucrats to be a new source of economic development. The instrumentalization of culture was distinctive in the Changdong, where the city government sought quick and tangible evidences of success before building partnerships with artists and local merchants. Artists and cultural agencies tried to counteract the government's move, but they were fragmented and marginalized. On the other hand, the Totatogaa case provides an example in which artists and local activists took the lead in conceptualizing culture and implementing it in a local context. The strong solidarity among artists and the city government's rather non – interventionist attitude were conducive generating more positive results. Certainly, merchants were commonly sidelined in all three projects, but unlike the other two cases, the Totagoga case demonstrated that merchants were taken into account from the inception, and they actually became cooperative as the project moved on.

From the three cases, the author argued that cultural districts can be sustainable and vitalized only with the active participation of private actors such as artists, art associations and cultural agencies. Just like illustrated in the Totatoga case, strong activism and the commitment of local artists were decisive factors in differentiating the consequences. In a fundamental sense, creativity comes from social interaction among civil actors who are free from government and commercial control (Stern and Seifert, 2007). Social bond, identity and shared value play an important role in creative place making. Thus, cultivating and nurturing civil actors should be considered as precondition for successful cultural district operation. However, the study believed that it doesn't mean that the role of government is not important. Rather than, in East Asia including Korea where government at national and local level has long exercised

Chapter Two Literature Review

dominant power over civil society, government still remains as an initial mover and a pattern setter. At the same time, city government should learn how to communicate with different local actors, such as artists and activists, and how to build horizontal and flexible governance with these actors. The author still believe that there is a big gap between the promotion of culture as a tool for economic development and the emerging of cultural place as creative milieu through diverse social processes. While civil organizations and cultural activists understand culture as shared values embedded in local community, entrepreneurial city government tend to focus on the instrumental aspect of culture for urban regeneration. Probably, this is an enduring source of conflict between government – led and culture – led urban regeneration strategies.

Ann Markusen and Anne Gadwa (2009) raised up an interesting research issue about arts and culture in urban or regional planning by putting through a review of cultural planning literature. Their study mainly reviews the "state of knowledge about arts and culture as an urban or regional development tool, exploring norms, reviewing evidence for causal relationships and analyzing stakeholders, bureaucratic fragmentation and citizen participation in cultural planning. Two strategies designed cultural districts and tourist – targeted cultural investments illustrate how better research would inform implementation. In guiding urban cultural development, researchers should examine and clarify the impacts, risks and opportunity costs of various strategies and the investments and revenue and expenditure patterns associated with each, so that communities and governments avoid squandering 'creative city' opportunities". One of issue about cultural planning mentioned by the authors is "the planning realms, cultural planners, who include for our purpose all policy makers and professionals engaged in the fostering of arts and cultural activity, base their strategies and prescriptions on one or more implicit norms that are linked to goals, stated or unstated. These norms reflect community values and since communities are diverse and encompass conflicting interests, such values may be multiple and disparate. Most cultural planning efforts to date fail to clearly state their underlying norms and related goals in ways that can be monitored, thereby handicapping researchers in their efforts to evaluate cultural planning initiatives (Evans, 2005). Given these acknowledged limitations, the study examines what norms and goals are evident in the relevant literature". The author also suggested that all city and regional cultural planning initiatives should begin with an explicit statement of the several *norms* that form their rationale and related *goals*. Not only are transparent norms and goals good government practice; they enable researchers to more effectively evaluate the success of an initiative. The study showed that very few cultural planning research efforts attempt to understand these norms or to develop measures that will gauge their performance such as economic impact studies of various arts and cultural investments are plagued with unwarranted assumptions and inference problems, therefore, researchers should unpack, critique and evaluate outcomes according to norms and goals. The author also emphasized importance of the roles of city cultural structure and external stakeholders to present a framework for understanding how cultural planning currently operates at the local level, examining variations in public sector cultural capacity and implementation as well as in the range and differing interests and power of stakeholders in cultural districts. By taking two examples of cultural district and cultural tourism to explore the goals, logic and evidence on outcomes, point out the poverty of good research with a question of "should cities and states designate and develop cultural districts where cultural activities are clustered together? Or should they encourage a decentralized mosaic of cultural activities throughout neighborhoods and among a series of small towns in a region? Finally, the study gives four areas of inquiry as crucial opportunities for researchers to strengthen understanding of cultural planning theory and practice, it could be showed by diagram as follow:

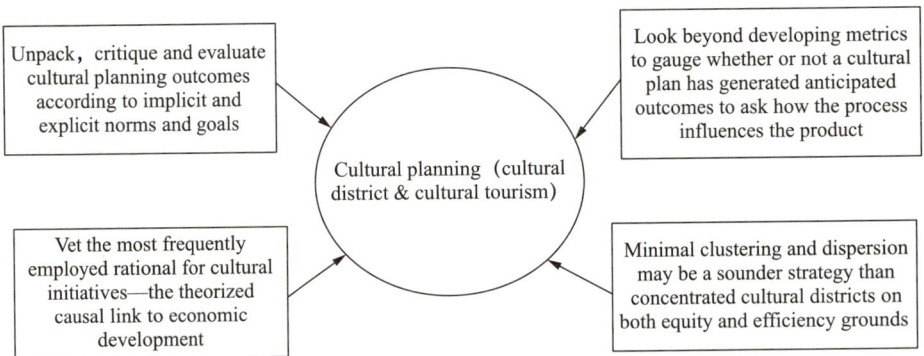

Diagram 2　Elements of a Cultural Planning Research Agenda

To sum up, according to this study the authors actually raise up a thinking way for evaluating the cultural planning. Decision maker often favor ephemeral tourists over their own residents as patrons, over – invest in large – scale arts facilities that may become expensive white elephants in the longer run, focus on particular districts rather than the mosaic of offerings that already exist, and fail to build decision – making frameworks where artists, smaller scale arts organizations, and a multiplicity of distinctive cultural communities can participate in cultural planning. It also showed us the attention of how to successfully develop a cultural project such as cultural district and cultural tourism.

Because recent literature has emphasized the importance of culture and the complementarities between culture and local tangible and intangible assets, Pier Luigi Sacco, Guido Ferilli, Giorgio Tavano Blessi, And Massimiliano Nuccio (2013) provide an analytical foundation for these processes with a view to developing tools for policy design, analysis and evaluation. By so called "system – wide cultural districts", it refers to a new approach to local development where cultural production and participation present significant strategic complementarities with other production chains. The authors believed that culture drives the accumulation of intangible assets such as human, social, and cultural/symbolic capital, thereby fostering economic and social growth and environmental sustainability. Recent studies (Cheng, 2006) emphasize the parallels between industrial and cultural "atmospheres" in these new development processes, the shift from industrial to cultural district implies a substantial change: Whereas the industrial district model is focused upon decentralized, vertical integration, and the cultural district model emphasizes horizontal integration (Pertto and Connolly, 2007). They also isolated 12 factors that can be associated with the capacity of cultural district facilitate the local system and economy. Although their works did not study such as mechanism of cultural district, mode of cultural district intervention and marketing mix etc, this emphasis on the structural role of culture in development dynamics calls for a different notion of a cultural districts, which is no longer limited to the activities of cultural players, but rather includes the capacity of culture to activate positive feedback dynamics that enhance the local system's capacity to produce, circulate, access information, and symbolic content. At the same time, the authors also analyse five case studies that can be taken as prototypes of the system – wide cultural district culture – led developmental model through comparing five cities in Europe and the U.S. They argued that System – Wide Cultural District (SWCD) is not simply a driving sector of the local economy but assumes a much more strategic function as a platform of innovation, social cohesion, and soft power. This analysis employs the 12 – factor model described in the companion paper to investigate the specific mix of dimensions—namely quality, development, attraction, sociality and networking. In spite of the differences in terms of their environments, economies, and cultures, a powerful common trait that runs throughout their developmental narratives is that in order for growth to occur, the local social dynamics of the production and transmission of knowledge must cease to be sector specific and become system wide. Finally, the study believed it is clearly difficult to look for "recipes" for successful culture - led development dynamics in a few simple rules, however contextualized, but a common theme seems to be the construction of dense, solid networks that allow local actors to join forces around a common developmental vision, therefore, the SWCD framework may be useful to discuss these issues and to articulate why and how there is both a need and an opportunity for a new generation of "smart" cultural policies to restart the engine of growth.

Antoine Le Blanc (2010) studied the cultural district by taking example of the South - East Cultural District in Sicily. The author believed that the industrialization of cultural production and a strong trend for the development of regional networks have recently led to the creation of new spatial and economic forms called "cultural districts", these new economic systems rely on very different geographical bases, types of products, and developmental processes. Although a specific form of spatial organization, the newly created South - East Cultural District, is based on cultural and architectural similarities, it is confronted with major obstacles such as economic heterogeneity, a lack of innovation and physical distance between the towns. Actually, this study pointed out those factors that affect a cultural district successfully develop mentioned above.

Mark J. Stern and Susan C. Seifert (2009) examined an alternative use of the arts for community development: Cultivating neighborhood *cultural cluster (district)* with modest concentrations of cultural providers, resident artists and cultural participants. It also presented innovative methods for integrating data on these indicators into a geographic information system to produce a Cultural Asset Index that can be used to identify census block groups with the highest density of these assets. This study proposed a way of thinking about cultural districts as organically linked to the economic and social life of cities and their neighborhoods. The author argued that culture can revive urban economies, not by placing a shiny veneer over crumbling decay, but by using the arts to engage community residents and revitalize their neighborhoods. The article explored the role that cultural district have played in spurring the revitalization of Philadelphia neighborhoods. The authors believe that the artists have become social entrepreneurs, selling their vision as well as their wares. They draw upon the variety of the world's traditions as well as the distinctive rhythms of the contemporary city. Thus, though the arts are commerce, they revitalize cities not only through their bottom - line but also through their social role. The author created a method that use a called Cultural

Asset Index (CAI) to aggregates data on a number of dimensions of cultural engagement and data on cultural participants, resident artists, nonprofit cultural organizations and commercial cultural firms are incorporated into a Geographic Information System (GIS) aggregated at the census block group level. The main purpose of using such an innovative method is to maximizing the revitalization effects of cultural assets agglomeration by cultivating neighborhood clusters and linking them through social equity and workforce development policy with the regional creative economy. According to the research, the author concluded: The first, there is a clear rationale for social investment. Given the significant positive externality associated with cultural clusters, investment strategies that are profit – seeking, not necessarily profit – maximizing, could pay huge dividends to both the investors and the general community. Small loans for predevelopment and bridge financing, especially if linked to technical assistance, could increase the success rate of individual enterprises and clusters in general; the second, the public sector can contribute to the viability of cultural clusters (districts) simply by doing its job better. Providing security, clean and safe streets, usable public spaces, convenient transit, and consistent and honest enforcement of zoning and development regulations would make the world much easier for those trying to seed and cultivated cultural cluster (districts). Strategic grants for place – making activities – such as distinctive street – scape and lighting, community and park facilities, and local fairs or festivals – would also provided returns greater than their costs; the third, urban economic policy makers should explore workforce development strategies that provide young people interested in the creative and cultural industries with the information and resources to make good decisions about entering the fields; finally, we need planners and researchers to help refine our statistical tools for monitoring the life history of cultural clusters (district). Cultivating cultural clusters can be but one approach to community planning and regional economic development policy. However, given their potential for generating social benefits beyond purely commercial success as well as their strategic importance to the health of a city and region's creative economy, nurturing neighborhood cultural cluster (district) is a strategy that deserves the attention of government, philanthropy and the private sector. It is obvious that the study mainly focus on assessing how much degree the cultural district can make contribution for the regional development and neighborhood revitalization through producing a so called Cultural Asset Index.

Cheng – Yi Lin and Woan – Chiu Hsing (2008) explored the role of community mobilization in Taipei's culture – led urban regeneration process by analyzing the case of the Bao – an Temple area. The study argued that the generation and use of cultural resources in urban regeneration lie in community mobilization and institutional support, rather than in a state – led cultural flagship approach, and the author concluded that local government needs to move beyond the instrumentalism of urban cultural strategies and to rediscover the spaces where local cultural activities and mobilization capacities are attached. Only through understanding the relationship between place and community mobilization will a virtuous cycle for the revitalization of a unique and historical urban area be generated.

Table 5 Hypothesis Impact & Indicator Used

Hypothesized Impact	Indicators Used
1. Cultural districts increase income	*Income*—log of median household annual income
	Poverty—percent of population under 150 percent of poverty
2. Cultural districts reduce unemployment, bring jobs to the area	*Employment*—percent of families with working adults
	Travel Time—average commute time in minutes
3. Cultural districts retain residents, stabilize neighborhoods	*Renters*—percent of households renting
	Stayers—percent of population in same residence 5 + years
4. Cultural districts local population, change the demographic mix	*PopDensity*—log of population density
	White—percent of population that is White
5. Cultural districts increase property values	*Prop Values*—log of median housing price
6. Cultural districts attract more educated	*College*—percent of adults with college degrees

Douglas S. Noonan (2013) briefly describes the phenomenon of cultural districts in the USA, reviews some claims made about their impacts, and provides evidence of districts' effect. Neighborhood – level statistical analyses identify socioeconomic trends in neighborhoods affected by districts. The results reflect the heterogeneity in cultural districts and in cities' experiences with them. The findings inform policies supporting creative place making in general and cultural districts as a system. Firstly, the author reviewed the literatures of studying cultural districts in USA it shows that cultural districts' sustainability is another concern, in light of the recent sever recession. Other drawbacks include the opportunity costs of supporting the concentrated investment. Displacing and disrupting more "organic" or decentralized cultural production and

Chapter Two Literature Review

consumption may create "losers" in the process; secondly, the study use empirical approaches to light on the US cultural district phenomenon, the neighborhoods nearby, and how districts influenced their demographic and economic trends. It has to say that the author used an innovative approach of making hypothesized impact and indicator used to test the influence for economic trends as follow:

In this table, along with each claim or expected impact are one or more indicators in the right – hand side column. The empirical analysis proceeds in two phases in order to measure impacts. The first phase is simply to assess the average demographic conditions and trends inside and outside of districts; the second phase refines the neighborhood comparison to leverage within – city variation in neighborhood trajectory and control for additional observed and unobserved factors. Through the process of analyzing, the study concluded that there is new evidence on the impact of cultural district in general. It is forming cultural districts that have consistently significant effects on population, education, race, families with children or distance to employment. It also revealed significant positive effects of district formation on property values, employment and income. However, this study cannot indicate whether any particular district is a success or failure, no matter its goals and the critical question of what makes for successful arts districts simply cannot be answered satisfactorily without understanding why some districts fail to process past the proposal stage or why some cities do not even entertain the proposal. The author points out in further that more and better data on additional districts and urban centers, and more sophisticated models, are needed to assess whether particular attributes of cities or districts engender success. Although research by Montgomery (2003) offers some theory and case studies to test for elements that make districts successful, case study approaches are limited in their generic perspective. On the other hand, given the enormous attention to, popularity of, and investment in cultural districts, therefore, more effort is needed to systematically collect data and to carefully analyze American cites' experiences with cultural districts.

Davide Ponzini, Silvia Gugu, Alessandra Oppio (2014) provided an overview of cultural districts in Italy explaining the contextual characteristics and constraints. The study draws on two in – depth case studies: One mainly focus on cultural mapping and the other on policy intervention. The authors maintain that it is not appropriate to use the concept as an analytical unit as well as a ready – made policy measure, at least with reference to Italy. Significant distinction should be made since the cultural district model has high explicable relevance but it needs to be reconsidered as a policy instrument. The case of the Veneto and Lombardy Regions and their comparison are relevant to both the national and international debates:

Both have a regional scope and show peculiar spatial features and governance dynamics:

Have different promoters: One project is carried out by the Regional Government and one by a nonprofit organization;

Target both urban and rural CDs (while most of the international debates considers urban environments only);

Show peculiar features of Italian interpretation of and experimentation with CDs;

Provide concrete examples of two different approaches to CDs, one has mainly developed analytical instruments and the other financing policy measures according to analyses and interaction with local stakeholders;

Have a strong knowledge base for detecting CDs and for programming new interventions.

Base on these debates, the two initiatives for CDs in Veneto and Lombardy show peculiar spatial features and political dynamics that reflect two distinct approaches to regional CDs in Italy. A fundamental difference between them is the conceptualization of the very notion of the CD, which impacted the cultural mapping process and the policy measures involved. Therefore, this study illustrated the facets of this particular problem in the Italian context, and highlights the distinctions between the two different acceptations of CD under several aspects, across two different cases: Policy goals, analytical approach, process management, and policy instruments and point out several key conclusions. Firstly, this topic is given considerable attention in national policy making in Europe – though it has a high territorial variety according to the specific geographical context and policy contents – without any clear reference to specific research and policy traditions. Secondly, this paper contributes to the debate with an in-depth study of two CD initiatives in Italy, providing evidence of and directing the attention towards the difference between two acceptations of CD under different perspectives (goals, analytical process, etc.). Thirdly, the mapping undertaken in the two cases showed that the knowledge produced relied on different paths, and the types of information and their relevance for action depended on an a priori conceptualization of CDs, rather than specific policy goals alone. The comparison of the two initiatives also makes it evident that complex cultural mapping can be achieved by policymakers without systematically involving local stakeholders (Arnaboldi & Spiller,

2011). Fourthly, regarding the prominent role of experts in cultural policy making, the high competence in cultural heritage matters and the prompt translation of an analytical concept such as the district into cultural policy guidelines have clearly been a two – edged sword for Italy. Fifthly, CD policy displays its development effects in the long term.

Eleonora Lorenzini (2010) seeks to identify the distinctive variables of a particular type of local production system: The extra – urban cultural district (E – UCD). The study think that cultural districts are becoming an important field of investigation, but most of the literature has concentrated on urban clusters, cities of art and cities of culture. Through drawing on research on the three Italian case studies of Cinque Terre, Vald'Orcia and Ravello, the author identified the three levers whose valorization determines the success of the development of the E – UCD. The E – UCD is a development model diffused above all in Mediterranean countries, such as Italy, Spain and France. It is not exclusively rural, since it contains small towns, usually significant in terms of heritage and tradition. Finally, this case study concluded that the main specificity of E – UCDs with respect to the other kinds of local production system is the centrality of integration among sectors for the development process. In particular, it has been highlighted that a process of valorization is based on specific resources of *tangible and intangible kind*. It often begins as the result of a spontaneous agglomeration, but the initiative of one or more local leaders in crucial to elaborate a strategy and win the consensus of other stakeholders. The development process is sustainable when based on community involvement, investment attraction and start – ups, innovation, integration among sectors and quality. Public authorities, agencies and super – local bodies can influence the path of development of their territories with their policies and intervention. On the other hand, this study has also demonstrated the importance of social capital in strengthening institutions' authority and the importance of institutions in strengthening social capital. In a word, this study demonstrated that the E – UCD is a model of sustainable development and an emerging destination for tourists, assuring at the same time a good quality of life for citizens and the valorization of cultural resources and quality products.

Won Bae Kim (2011) discussed the strategy of cultural district development in Seoul. Through two cases of Insadong and Daehagno are taken to examine several issues concerning inherent conflicts between culture and commerce, the way culture and tradition is perceived and interpreted by different groups, and the focus of cultural strategy. The viability of cultural districts is discussed in terms of governance, policy goals and measures and programming needs. In particular, the author argued that, although a collaborative form of governance is desired in general, its sustainability is questionable unless there exist critical discourses reformulating the meaning of culture and tradition and searching the best means to balance culture and commerce. The author introduced the historic development of the two cultural districts in Seoul and identifies the successful factors for the two districts. The study described the viability of cultural district strategy in Seoul in further on three perspectives: *Policy goals and measures of the official cultural district strategy, the effects of cultural district designation and different focuses and programming needs for Insadong and Daehagno*. Finally, the author concluded that the cultural district strategy of Seoul is obviously a recent addition, which has grown out of public consciousness about culture and tradition. Even though it still needs further refinements, the cultural district strategy can be considered as a significant step forward by the public authority involving in urban cultural strategy. It suggest that the effectiveness and mode of public involvement, managing conflicts between culture and commerce, and the relationship between place and activity need to be addressed in the future. Firstly, those social actors can question about the effectiveness of public involvement in cultural district management; secondly, there exists a more fundamental issue of inherent conflict between commerce and culture or more specifically profit – motivation and cultural regeneration; finally, the foregoing discussion leads to the conceptual and practical problem of cultural district strategy, for example, the relationship between activity and place, what these actors want to preserve and promote: Cultural activity or place? In a word, it is difficult to develop common programs for cultural districts and the role of the public sector is inherently limited in programming activities since most cultural activities are carried out by the private sector. On the other hand, the author believed that the private – public partnership suggest here in the management of cultural districts does not mean that conflicts and contradictions between culture and commerce will be resolved by such a partnership. The tendency of commoditization traditional culture in Insadong and smearing performing arts in Daehagno by commercial interests has been seen. These tendencies, which are unavoidable in the market – driven processes of urban development, can only be mitigated by critical cultural discourses among community organization and local citizens. The study also realized that non – government and non – profit organizations can take a lead in generating such discourses as exemplified in the case of Insadong and Daehagno, in order to improve the

Chapter Two Literature Review

effectiveness of cultural district strategy, the goals and programs of cultural district strategy need to be carefully developed to tailor the specific context of a cultural district and the results need to be regularly evaluated with multiple sets of criteria representing the full spectrum of views on cultural and its meaning.

Hilary Anne Frost – Kumpf (2001) in the PHD dissertation examines the growing phenomena of cultural districts as a strategy of urban development in the United States. The author rose up three questions: ①How are cultural districts formed and what is their morphology (physical form, plan, functional areas)? ②What patterns and typologies of cultural district formation and morphology can be seen by comparing and contrasting cultural districts? ③What are the ideologies of urban development and arts management that are influencing cultural district development? Firstly, the distinct formation, morphology and management structures of cultural district in the United States have been described. The local community leadership and their motivations and concerns for revitalization and arts development have influenced the formation of these cultural districts. Three primary instigators for cultural district development have been proposed: Artists and arts organizations, local growth coalitions, and downtown business associations. It will be argued that each of these groups has influenced the development of specific cultural district morphologies with varying focuses on arts consumption and production activities. However, one way of understanding the resulting morphology of cultural districts is to better understand the ideology that underlies their development. Secondly, the author explored the underlying frameworks that may influence the development ideology of some of the players in cultural district formation. It suggest that both arts organizations and local growth coalitions may find that gentrification and public art attract desirable audience members, and may choose to include these aspects in cultural district development. But some arts organizations, and especially local arts agencies that are interested in broad democratic involvement by all audiences in arts activities, may be troubled by the development of facilities that presume some kind of elite cultural capital for their consumption. These groups may therefore create cultural districts that, through broad focus on arts production and arts consumption, and diverse choices of arts and entertainment, increase the likelihood of wider community participation in the district. Thirdly, it explored how local growth coalitions, arts organizations, and downtown business associations have channeled their ideologies of urban development in the creation of cultural district in the United States. The results showed that there are important differences in the kinds of cultural districts found in cities in the United States. It illustrated the three actors different focus for cultural districts growth. Most of the districts created by local growth coalitions are focused on high arts consumption, driven by an ideology of creating spaces that will attract visitors to the district and the city, and in creating a place that will promote elite images for the city; arts organizations seem to create both consumption and production focused districts, depending on local needs, but responding to the need for service to arts organizations and arts as the first priority. They also, in most case, appear to create districts with a focus in high arts activities; downtown business associations, responding to their own interests for business development, seem to create broadly focused arts and entertainment consumption districts. Even the author created a formula: Cultural spaces/activities + redevelopment = success for the arts and the city. Overall, this study has documented the scope and diversity of cultural districts in the United States, particularly providing details about cultural district formation, morphology and management. By drawing from the literature in urban studies and arts management, frameworks for understanding the possible ideologies determining cultural district development have been presented. Of particular interest in this study are the cultural district preferences of the primary leadership groups that have lead cultural district formation: Local growth coalitions, arts organizations, and downtown development organizations and their diverse interests in consumption versus production, and high culture versus arts and entertainment.

Anna Maria Bounds (2006) took the example of Philadelphia's cultural district to examine how leaders from government, arts and business worked together to implement the cultural district, the Avenue of the Arts, as a strategy for generating tourism and reviving a declining downtown area by drawing on network management scholarship. This case study analyzed the implementation of fifteen cultural district projects, with particular focus on the network leadership. The case study evaluated how each key stakeholder led the network through organizing interest, building consensus and utilizing policy tools to achieve the network's goals. The finding are contrasted with theories that claim a network is either managed by a single actor who directs it or is self-organized, in which mutual adjustment of network actors enables collective goals. This study suggests network management is a process in which multiple leaders "steer" as a network evolves, and requires different leaders—who utilize different skills and interventions related to their social position—to be successful. Through identifying outcomes of the initiative, analyzing the role of network management in implementation, and determining the most effective network manager, the study found that all successful

Chapter Two Literature Review

projects benefited from network managers who brought new actors to the project, engaged in problem solving, and facilitated interactions within the network, conversely, most failed projects lacked a network manager and were undermined by weak organizational leadership. On the other hand, the success of projects also was influenced by geographical location on Broad Street. South Broad Street projects benefited from their Center City location and proximity to cultural attractions. Network managers also supported them, as the network's primary objective and North Broad Street projects failed because the area lacked an agglomeration of cultural facilities, the proposed projects were not venues or arts-based, and their largely black leadership lacked political power. Thus, network managers did not attempt to re-direct the network's resources toward this component of the initiative. As to the finding of the study, firstly it suggest that network management is a process in which multiple leaders "steer" at different stages, that is, there is not a single manager, as a network evolves, it requires different leaders to achieve success; secondly, each key actor leads a network by utilizing different types of skills and interventions related to their social positions. The study more emphasize on the importance of network management playing a significant role in the success of project and the role of network managers' strength in a successful projects because network managers brought new actors and resources to the project, engaged in problem solving, and facilitated positive interactions within the network, conversely, the majority of failed projects lacked a network manager, and have a weak organizational leadership undermined the success of projects. The literature related to cultural district could be summarized by table as follow:

Table 6 Summary Research of Western Countries

Perspectives	Focus	Resources
Urban & region regeneration; local development; regional economic development	Focus on the necessity of endowing local economies with a cultural infrastructure; five cases taken as prototype SWCD	Pier Luigi Sacco, Guido Ferilli, et al. (2013) "Culture as an engine of local development process: System-wide culture district: Prototype cases"
	Developing body of theory on cultural districts in extra-urban areas	Eleonora Lorenzini (2010). "The extra-urban cultural district: An emerging local production system: Three Italian Case Studies"
	Provide an analytical foundation for these processes with a view to developing tools for policy design, analysis and evaluation	Pier Luigi Sacco, Guido Ferilli et al. (2013) "Culture as an engine of local development processes: System-wide cultural districts: Theory"

continued table

Perspectives	Focus	Resources
Urban & region regeneration; local development; regional economic development	Exploring norms, reviewing evidence for causal relationships, and analyzing stakeholders, bureaucratic fragmentation, and citizen participation in cultural planning	Ann Markusen and Anne Gadwa (2009) "Art and culture in urban or regional planning: A review and research agenda"
	Examining an alternative use of the arts for community development to product a Cultural Asset Index that can be used to identify census block groups with the highest density of these assets	Mark J. Stern and Susan C. Seifert (2009) "Cultural clusters: The implications of cultural assets agglomeration for neighborhood revitalization"
	Mainly assesses the hypothesis that public investments in the arts can spur local development, and the implication for the choices over which are the most effective public investments if the hypothesis is true	Michael Rushton (2013) "Cultural districts and economic development in American cities"
	Overcoming these obstacles such as economic heterogeneity, a lack of innovation, and physical distance between the towns; try to create synergies and in integrating other economic sectors	Antoine Le Blanc (2010) "Cultural districts, a new strategy for regional development? The south-east cultural district in Sicily"
	Exploring the complex relationships between contemporary development discourses and historically embedded postcolonial subjectivities and policy legacies	Mike Raco, Katherine Gilliam (2011) "Geographies of abstraction, urban entrepreneurialism, and the production of new cultural spaces: The West Kowloon cultural district, Hong Kong"
	Exploring the role of community mobilization in Taipei's culture-led urban regeneration process by analyzing the case of the Bao-an Temple area	Cheng-Yi Lin and Woan-Chiau Hsing (2008) "Cultural-led urban regeneration and community mobilization: The case of the Taipei Bao-an temple area, Taiwan"
	Broaden knowledge on policy governance of cultural districts, particularly those utilizing artist communities for urban revitalization	Se Hoon Park (2015) "Can we implant an artist community? A reflection on government-led cultural districts in Korea"
	Describe the phenomenon of cultural districts; identify socioeconomic trends in neighborhoods affected by district	Douglas S. Noonah (2013) "How US cultural districts reshape neighborhoods"

Chapter Two Literature Review

continued table

Perspectives	Focus	Resources
Evolution of cultural district	The history of New York's creative districts from Greenwich Village in the early 1900s to Bushwick today shows that the unanticipated consequences of unplanned	Sharon Zukin, Laura Brashow (2011) "The life cycle of New York's creative districts: Reflections on the unanticipated consequences of unplanned cultural zones"
Policymaking	Focus on cultural mapping and the other on policy intervention; cultural district model need to be reconsidered as a policy instrument	Davide Ponzini, Silvia Gugu, Alessandra Oppio (2014) "Is the concept of the cultural district appropriate for both analysis and policymaking? Two case in Northern Italy"
	The strategy of cultural district development in Seoul	Won Bae Kim (2011) "The viability of cultural districts in Seoul"
Mechanism of cultural project or districts	Focus on the debate by investigating the micro-level interactions among stakeholders during conceptualization of a large collaborative project	Michela Arnaboldi, Nicola Spiller (2010) "Actor-network theory and stakeholder collaboration: The case of cultural districts"

From above the summary of literature we can see that the most of articles more focus on the urban and region regeneration, local development, and regional economic development. Other articles respectively focus on evolution of cultural district, policy making and mechanism of cultural project or districts. In these articles cultural districts are described as a considerable component to affect and stimulate the urban or regional economic development, it also become a instrument of decision making. However, there are few articles for the research of the mechanism of cultural project or districts.

3. Researches in Domestic

At the end of last century, some researchers begin to develop the study for the issues related to culture in domestic. At that time, the term of cultural district are more understood as *cultural cluster, art zones and creative area etc*. The study will review

· 41 ·

those contributions and try to find the current situations of researches (the *term cultural district will be used in this study*).

Liu mingliang (2010) took the example of 798 cultural districts in Beijing to explore and analyze the mutual relationship between inside of cultural district and external social environment through anthropology and sociology statistical methods under the globalization and market. The study suggests that the art zone and artist village is a special cultural phenomenon which appeared in 1990s in China. It is an area where gathered by a group of professional painters at the very first beginning, then many galleries enter into here and commercial factor affected this area, these factors lead to artists to leave this area and move to 798 district. As a case of field study, 798 district not only with its own structure and feature but also affected by many factors which come from domestic and foreign country in politics, culture & art market and it's structure that is changed with these factors. The external environment of 798 cultural district show the state of multiple symbiosis, each factor is mutual independent and premise in this art group. The different factors are connected by the market and formed a whole art ecology environment, and became a complicated interactive chain. The development of 798 district is affected by many factors that affect its appearing because it is the result of the interaction of those different level factors and stakeholders.

On the other hand, the change and difficulties appeared in 798 district embodies the whole state and art ecology, which appeared in the period of social and cultural transformation in China. The artist group in China is a kind of unique cultural and art phenomenon which is appeared by social and cultural transformation in China. This group is appearing and develop with Chinese contemporary art. In a sense, the change history of Chinese art group and artist "Migration history", actually it is a kind of history of Chinese Contemporary art – From "Underground" to "Ground", also from "Marginal" to "Mainstream". In the view of art market, the change in 798 districts is a progress of constructing and deconstructing in the context of market; in the context of globalization, it is a integration progress of eastern and western culture and art or a cultural competition. It is well know, 798 districts was grown from an abandoned factory and become a most famous art district in China, it features that the popular force begin to overtake early idealism period for Utopia pursuit, it begin to combined the art pursuit with contemporary social and people, and in the pursuit of its own discourse. The idea and action of "rebuild" the open and public state, which is not only feature with prominent advancement, and also feature with positive practice: This is make the early contemporary art step out of the state of "Underground" and small circle and also find a practical way for contemporary. However, 798 districts also face the double pressure from domestic and foreign country, it reflect the plight of Chinese immature art market. The mature art market should be established and contemporary art will have its local place in the competition.

Zhang tianyu (2013) mainly focus on the contemporary art in the means of anthropology, although the traditional research form, that is, artistic ontology, was not first utilized for the contemporary art, meanwhile, on the basis of the attention and methodology, the research method combined with anthropology, sociology, fine arts, art theory, economics and statistics was not also its first utilization, such entries to concentrate on the ecological situation of artistic community, spectrum relationship between each other, relation network between groups, also comparison, mutual help, conflict, integration linking the internal and external, the analysis of the ecological system and cultural context of art community, together with the causes and appearance of the community environment, will be conducive to put forward protection measures, then further, by analyzing the art community and combining the above mentioned information, the summary of the back story and crucial reasons of the contemporary art back from the macroscopic view will be the featuring and creative points of the research.

Huang bin (2010) integrates the theoretical framework of the interaction of microstructure evolution and spatial evolution to present the idea that industry cluster will determine the spatial concentration in Beijing. Industrial cluster depends on external (convenience of the city and the related industrial base) and internal components (especially the innovation network). The formation of industrial cluster determine the path of dependence through elastic specialized division of labor, and then moving towards economies of scale and scope of economic development, will further enhance differentiate, or creatively destruct industrial clusters. This study systematically combined the internal and external components (including policy conditions) of Beijing to develop cultural and creative industries. The author found that cultural and creative industrial in Beijing are obvious to the professional development trend, self – association and self – growth trend of industry has increased. Among which the high – tech industrial clusters are formed by information transmission, computer services and software industry. The three leading industrial clusters in cultural and creative industries contact each other mainly through leasing and business services. Subsequently, the study selects 13 factors affecting the development of cultural and creative industrial. The paper takes 13 districts and counties of Beijing as analyzing object, uses the panel data of 2006 – 2010 to make a regression analysis, and it combines the case studies of typical cultural and creative industries areas to the influencing factors of the spatial selection of cultural and creative industries and its development. The analysis shows that the public library circulation is a most important indicator of the cultural and creative industries, other important factors includes the add – valued of the servers industries except cultural and creative industries. The case study also shows the key role such as contingency, central figure and social networks have played in the formation of industrial clustering. Finally, the study concludes that the space evolution of Beijing cultural and creative industries and the case conforms with the mutual influence of industry and space, and suggested the adjusting direction and further research direction of Beijing cultural and creative industries.

Although Xiao yanfei (2007) did not particularly focused on cultural districts, the study explored the dynamic mechanism and innovation models of development of economic spaces of creative industrial district which related to cultural districts issues. The study explored new area of the creative industrial district. Firstly, it includes spatial approach into the main research points on creative industrial district, analyzing the dynamic factors and relation form theory of the economic space, and point out that the local labor market, creative talents, local culture, creative milieu, the impelling of new economy and the function of government are the most important dynamic factors, and these factors constitutes a network relation multidimensional diffusion by the new economic theory of alternative space. Secondly, it considers creative industrial district as a innovative space, analyzing the function of regional development and innovation, dynamic mechanism and models, the models of spatial innovation, with the concludes of three dynamic models that are gradual advance model, frog – jump model and cooperative model and four models of space innovation that are spatial shifted model, value inter – linkage model, interactive growth model and system integrated model. And, thirdly, it considers the creative industrial district as a complex self – organization system, analyzing the dynamic mechanism of interior and exterior effect of the system, with the character of self – intensification and limitless innovation of system revolution. Finally, the study concluded that creative industrial district is s called a "new economic spatial", it plays a key role for urban development and spatial innovation; creative industrial is fundamental basement of creative industrial districts, key points for the

Chapter Two Literature Review

debates of creative industrial concept is how to recode implication of creativity; it is important to define and analyze relative concepts of creative industrial, background and components; the investment for individual creativity and culture by creative district will be its origin for regeneration of new & old economy; creative districts has characteristics of complex system and self – organization; economic spatial of creative district includes labor market, creative talent and local culture which are related to new economic technology and government motivation.

Lou xiaoyan (2013) discussed industrial heritage's value, cultural & creative industries' characteristics and analyzed relationship between industrial heritage and cultural & creative industries. Then the study address the dynamic mechanism and theirs interaction in the formation and development of the cultural and creative industrial distinct which transform the industrial heritage, using the knowledge of experience economy theory, industrial agglomeration theory and evolution economic geography theory. Moreover, the author use the specific domestic case study to explore the evolution mechanism of the cultural and creative industrial district which transforms the industrial heritage. On the basis of theoretical analysis, the study tries to find out the key factors in the formation and development of the cultural and creative industrial district which transform the industrial heritage. Finally, empirical methods will be used to test and confirm the results. It concludes that the cultural and creative industrial distinct which transform the industrial heritage mainly defines a industry park that offers production, exchange, allocation and consumption of spiritual culture products and services by taking advantage of industrial heritage to discover the value of industrial heritage and to protect it; the study also found out the dynamic mechanism and analyses their impact on the development of the park. At the same time, this paper discusses the evolution rules and development pattern of this type of cultural and creative industrial district; finally, the author summaries the main influential factors of formation and development of the cultural and creative industrial district which transform the industrial heritage. It studies on the questionnaires from 49 enterprises in 5 this type of cultural and creative industrial district in Hangzhou and gets a conclusion that flexible labor, creative talent, creative environment, government support, competition and collaboration among enterprises and market demand are the main influential factors.

Jin wenting (2014) compared 798 art district in Beijing and the Insadong cultural district in Seoul. This study mainly focused on the subject of all interrelations in these two districts. "human" and conducts comprehensive study and analysis on the characteristics of these two districts. This paper pays more attention to the experiences, mentality and such levels of the users. Especially the "landscape" reappears as a kind of cultural visual image with the symbolic values in the sensation level based on human bodies, while "space" is studied through the individual experiences brought about by senses of various body movements. The two categories of "landscape" and "space" are the core arguments of this study. The symbolic meaning connects with the core problems of contemporary art history of China and South Korea. In the meantime, among the large number of urban spaces and venues involved in the scramble for capital in the post – industry age, it steals the thunder by its unique and charming characteristics. The study also argued that Chinese and Korea contemporary art histories, through the platform of art district, are truly shown in specific space by the visual reappearance of the landscape. The study also mentioned the concept of "interactivity", which is the brand new media environment and interactive art. This "interactivity" can be verified theoretically. Therefore, 798 art district and Insadong cultural district respectively representing the culture and arts of China and South Korea are firstly decomposed to numerous small venues according to our own physical experiences, and later recomposed to the mobile new space with our selection and activities. This is the decomposition and reconstruction of two artistic spaces the study argued. During this process, the "interactivity" can be realized and the artistic shared value can be practiced in the actual life.

Zhang lingyun (2012) mainly focus on those issues such as defining cultural district, measuring their economic benefits when they are as tools in local development, forming organizations of production and consumption sectors in the cultural districts, working mechanism of the cultural districts. Of which comprehensive economic benefits of the cultural districts in the Western countries is the most concerned, people are trying to measure their generated economic benefits through various channels. This research related to every stakeholder from western cultural districts as a comprehensive system study from both domestic and international perspectives. Based on related literature, and repeated consultation and advice from senior scholars of related areas of the western cultural districts, stakeholders about cultural districts were divided in this study to be as confining layer stakeholders and outer layer stakeholders. Those who are directly related to the cultural production and consumption are consumer groups, arts & culture groups of talented people and professional non – profit organization; and cultural production and

Chapter Two Literature Review

consumption policies, premises, facilities and funds associated with stakeholder groups are the government and its relevant departments, profitable business group of organizations and community residents and volunteer groups. This study also confirmed many success stories around the world, including the Stratford town, all year round to offer arts and culture activities, artistic performances and with art ever – changing forms, which is art " live in " community, coupled with appropriate support and guidance, thus cultural atmosphere informed as critical factors. The study also found that, due to advances in technology, the concept of formation from the traditional geographic concepts of cultural districts is expected to be broken through their geographical constraints, to be "virtual cultural district". This virtual cultural district will be very different from its rational form of organization, performing arts and management and geographical issues, and will be a great challenges and opportunities for every stakeholder. The study show that firstly, Western countries as United States, Canada, Uk's cultural districts fully fit for their urban economic development and processes, which meet their generally faced economic transfer needs, focusing on the domestic demand of the people on the art, but later it was gradually affected in turn noted by the culture economic value of the arts. Therefore, for the aspirations of the Western countries, there are two main routs about the cultural district development. The role of the cultural district in the urban economy is not as effective as the legendary and magical, more and more aware of the combined effect of the cultural district in the social environment and community life, rather than emphasizing only economic booster effect. Secondly, the big city landmark buildings in the development of urban culture and the arts, and even for the arts and culture atmosphere, have very limited role. The study found that a growing number of community people spontaneously participate in or organize the arts and cultural activities in all aspects, such as financial support, with proper policy support they are gradually become the tendency of the mainstream. Many cities and towns of the western countries has been extended arts organizations based mode to the life and scope of work of the communities, serving as an integral part of the recovery strategy. In addition, the author believe that as long as the sources of contributions, a large proportion of arts and culture closely related to the commercial corporate and private in western cultural district, on the other hand, non – profit organizations in cultural district their role are directly active in the arts and culture, such as financial preparation, artist information services etc. , they have played great roles. The culture atmosphere plays a vital role for the success of the cultural district.

This study confirms many success stories around the world, including the case of Stratford town, all year round to offer arts and culture activities, artistic performances and with art ever – changing forms, which is art "live in" community, coupled with appropriate support and guidance, thus cultural atmosphere informed as critical factors. The study also found that, due to advances in technology, the concept of formation from the traditional geographic concepts of cultural district is expected to be broken through their geographical constraints, to be "virtual cultural district". This virtual cultural district will be very different from its rational form of organization, performing arts and management and geographical issues, and will be a great challenges and opportunities for every stakeholder.

The author believed that no matter the series of stakeholders has truly played the roles, one successful model cannot always be special in the practice field, we should take into account of multiple factors in the merger process, as every place has special geographical characteristics, geographic range, and each containing different factors, different planning models, management and government agencies.

Zhang wang (2011) found that creative district and talent mainly assembled in north, eastern, northern and middle southern of China, it formed six biggest creative district clusters. Social capital, efficiency of financial market, creative capital, consumption preference and intelligent protection force are key attributes for development of creative industrial. Social capital and developed financial market system facilitate development of creative industrial. Because of the uncertainty relationship of creative capital and creative industrial, the storage of creative capital exceed a specific value, then it can lead to creative capital improve the development of creative industrial. By comparing the experiences of UK and America, the study classified model of creative industrial into two patterns: Market – orientation and government – orientation and compared differences of the two patterns on four perspectives such as leading forces, creativity origination, purpose and range of effectiveness. The author believed that creative industrial could be formed naturally only if the interests of creative firm's corporation exceed a critical value; on the other hand, the benefit of creative industrial can cover the cost of operation, creative districts could be supported by government. However, many researchers domestic made their own academic contributions to this issue related to culture district or culture industrial on different perspective, it could be summarized by table as follow:

Chapter Two Literature Review

Table 7 Summary of Literature Domestic

Theory	Focus	Resources
Industrial cluster theory; Experience economics; Economic geographic; Institutional economics	Cultural industrial policy, constructing theoretical framework for cultural industrial analysis according to the current situation of An Hui province in China	Cheng xiazhen (2014) "study on government support for the development of cultural industrial cluster in Anhui Province"
	To study the affective attributes and formation mechanism of cultural industrial agglomeration and analyze the agglomerative effectiveness of cultural industrial, innovative effectiveness and urban spatial redevelopment effectiveness base on the data of China cultural industrial	Yuan hai (2012) "Study for formation of cultural industrial agglomeration"
	To analyze the formative mechanism, emphasis on analyzing agglomerative distribution, productive network of cultural industrial cluster and interactive relationship between mutual – national corporation and cultural industrial cluster	Liu wei (2007) "Research for formative mechanism of cultural industrial cluster"
	Analyzing the relationship between industrial heritage and cultural creative industrial; exploring dynamic evolution mechanism and influence of industrial heritage; find out the attributes which affect the industrial heritage cultural creative district	Lou xiayan (2013) "A study on evolution of the cultural and creative industrial district which transforms from industrial heritage"
	To explore the regularities of Hu nan province cultural industrial spatial development and provide theoretical support for cultural industrial development and urban redevelopment	Dai yu (2012) "Study on spatial agglomeration of cultural industrial: A case study in Hunan province"
	Exploring the dynamic mechanism of cultural creative industrial spatial agglomeration through applying for industrial economics, spatial economics, and systematic dynamics	Sun jie (2012) "Study for agglomerative dynamic force mechanism of cultural creative industrial"
	Identifying the problems and attributes of cultural capital operation and cultural industrial development, then try to find out the approaches to solve these problems; constructing the operation pattern of cultural capital	Liu lijuan (2013) "Research on cultural capital operation and the development of cultural industry"
	Through comparing the differences between major cultural creative districts, use the successful experience of developed countries for exploring more suitable for China's cultural creative development pattern	Wu wei (2014) "Research on the interactive development between creative industries and regional economic growth"

continued table

Theory	Focus	Resources
Anthropology & Art; Statistics theory; Humanities	Providing evidence for government cultural industrial policies decision making	Zhang yali (2014) "Study on the development and path selection of cultural industry in China"
	To find the elements which affect the relationship of creative industrial and economic development such as creative atmosphere, creative talent etc.	Zhang wang (2011) "The research on China's developing modes of the cultural & creative industries"
	To analyze the mutual relationship between the inner zone and outside society through the case study of 798 cultural district	Liu mingliang (2010) "Beijing 798 Art Zone: Field study and follow-up study in the context of market"
	Base on the theory of comparison to analyze the cultural labor factors and explore the formation mechanism, systematic model and function pattern related to China cultural industrial core comparative advantage	Zhao yong (2014) "On the core comparative advantage of China's cultural industry with a fundamental strategy to participate in global competition"
	Focus on the contemporary art in the means of anthropology; ecological situation of artistic community, spectrum relationship between each other, relation network between groups	Huang bin (2010) "An evolution study of cultural & creative industries' space in Beijing"
	Focus on constructing the model of dynamic evolution for identifying the mechanism of cultural district agglomeration	Yan xiong (2014) "An analysis of national culture industry-cluster development in Lijiang"
	Development of creative industrial district depends on spatial innovation, new economic development and regeneration of urban functional space; focus on exploring dynamic mechanism and innovative model	Xiao yanfei (2007) "A study of the dynamic mechanism and innovation models of development of economic spaces of the creative industrial distric"
	Exploring western countries' cultural district stakeholders related to cultural districts by using of stakeholder theory	Zhang lingyun (2012) "Exploring stakeholders of culture districts in western countries: Stratford as a case in Canada"
	Through analyzing the case study of 798 cultural district and Insadong of Korea, not only focus on the people as a subject related to inside of district occurred but also users' experience and psychology	Jin wenting (2014) "A comparative study on the art & culture districts under the post-modern cultural context"

Chapter Two Literature Review

continued table

Theory	Focus	Resources
Anthropology & Art; Statistics theory; Humanities	To find out these problems which affect operation of artists and explore the grow path for lower & middle level artists' development	Fu ying (2012) "Research for Song zhuang art cluster operation"
		Zhang tianyu (2013) "The ecological study of art communities in Songzhuang Beijing"
	Explore how urban redevelopment drive the development of cultural industrial and try to summarize the experiences of western countries' urban regeneration for the practice of China's urban redevelopment and cultural industrial development, particular the latter	Zhang wei (2013) "Study of the culture industries development within the process of the urban regeneration in the West, as well as the illumination for China's practice"

From the summary, contrast to the research of western countries, more articles focus on basing on anthropology, art and humanity etc, other articles described cultural district on the view of industrial cluster, experience economy and economic geography. This study found that there are differences for cultural district research between western and domestic through literature review.

Both of them are seldom focus on researching the managerial mechanism and operation attributes of cultural district, those researchers did not deeply describe and analyze the cultural district itself as a system. Therefore, this study will develop the innovative research to identify the attributes and how to successfully operate cultural district.

4. Methodology

4.1 Theory Development

The first stage of research involves two intertwined tasks, developing the research question and selecting the overall research design. In addition to providing the conceptual structure of the study, this crucial stage also addresses important design questions such as case selection, defining units of analysis and data collection protocols. Developing a theoretical research question is an essential component of the study. As discussed earlier, case study is best suited for answering explanatory questions. Researching explanatory questions benefits from case study's examination of a phenomenon over time. A clear research question includes both an important theoretical question and points to relevant evidence. In these cases, a comprehensive literature review supplies both the theoretical foundations for the study and research models. For other cases, existing scholarship may not provide clear direction as the body of knowledge may be weak it may be an emerging field. Therefore, such case studies will be exploratory. In this event, the study must clearly define what is to be explored, its purpose, and the criteria by which the exploration will be judged successful.

Because case study research is a method of learning, designed to provide "concrete, practical, and context – dependent knowledge" (Flyvbjerg, 2001), the selection of a case for investigation is critical. Although the single case study is an appropriate research design in several circumstances (Hamel et al., 1994; Stake, 1995; Yin, 1994), in this study several case were selected for summarizing the common factors from different case and it is one of fundamental for theoretical analysis of the core successful factors for cultural district. However, a single case study may be utilized when it represents the critical case in testing a theory. On the other hand, the single case can also be used to confirm a theory or introduce alternative explanations. A single case study may also be used when a case represents an extreme or unique case. In addition, single case studies are sometimes used in the exploratory stage of an experimental study or as a pilot case in multiple – case research. A central misunderstanding of case study research is that one cannot generalize statistically on the basis of an individual case; therefore, the single case study cannot contribute to scientific development. However, the strength of this claim "depends upon the case one is speaking of, and how it is chosen" (Flyvbjerg, 2001).

4.2 Research Design of the Study

Case Selection

Three cases are selected in this study. They are Avenue of Arts in Philadelphia America, Insa – Dong Cultural District Korea and Seven – Nine – Eight Cultural District Beijing. Firstly, the Avenue of Arts initiative is considered a model case for city government participation in cultural district development and management (Brooks &

Chapter Two Literature Review

Kushner, 2001; Frost – Kumpf, 1998). The initiative's complexity and expansive nature, the proposed development of ten core projects involving the participation of diverse actors ranging from the state government to small local performing arts companies, allows for the investigation of network management in multiple contexts and level of organizations. The historical significance of both the city of Philadelphia and its major avenue South Broad Street provide an important context for studying network management by demonstrating how an elected city official engages in entrepreneurial use cultural assets to revitalize its downtown area. Secondly, the project of Daein Market in Gwangju City is the initiative's complexity and expansive nature, the proposed development of the core project involving the participation of diverse actors ranging from the state government to small local performing arts companies, allow for the investigation of network management in multiple contexts and levels of organizations. Thirdly, the historical significance of Seven – Nine – Eight cultural district Beijing provide an important context for identifying those actors and influencing attributes to cultural districts' successful operation.

In – depth Interview

In – depth interviewing was a primary component of this research. To develop an understanding of how key actors engaged in management and marketing decision making in Seven – Nine – Eight cultural district. To facilitate the unfolding of perspective, a questionnaire was used to suggest categories and topics to explore, leaving the possibility of discussing subjects introduced by the respondent. Test through an earlier pilot study, the questionnaire contained questions designed to provide information on the cultural district's development. In addition to the questionnaire, a topic guide was prepared for each interview to serve as an information resource during the interview and as a preliminary scheme for the analysis of transcripts. A topic guide is a summary of the potential key topics based on relevant readings, field research, and previous interviews (Gaskell, 2000). For each interview, a topic guide was prepared that outlined the development of the specific project organization, including key events and actors, important quotations from previous interviews, and a list of missing information or confusing details. The topic guides also worked as prompts during the interviews to aid in prompting respondents to recall specific details and as a reference for forming follow – up questions. Following the interviews, the topic guides were also used to analyze transcripts by comparing the respondent's viewpoint to archival research and other interviews.

Respondents included key actor involved in the initiative such as elected city government officials, directors of city government agencies, leaders of arts organizations and academics. Numerous informal interviews were also conducted with academic researchers and district visitors as opportunities arose such as at lectures, dinners, and research institutions. Given the impromptu nature of these interviews, interview notes were often hand – written rather than recorded and transcribed. In formal interviews involved two types of respondents, informants that I had met during the research process or other researcher completing work on other cultural projects. Both typed of informal interviews served as touchstones for my research because they provided me with the opportunity to consider my ideas in relation to different perspectives. Brief interviews with tourists on the Seven – Nine – Eight cultural district offer the chance to learn more about the nature of the district as destination for culture and entertainment.

Case Analysis

The analysis was guided by two research questions involving identifying the outcomes of the Avenue of the Arts initiative, Daein Art Market and Seven – Nine – Eight cultural district, assessing the role that those attributes play in the outcomes, and determine which were most effective factors based on network evaluation criteria. These questions were investigated by identifying each specific managerial activities strategy used by key actors and analyzing its related outcome. However, Seven – Nine – Eight cultural district was typically selected to explore the key issue related to consumers' behaviors and attitudes as marketing strategy evidence for decision making. To facilitate this investigation, interview data, archival research, and policy documents were triangulated to construct a chronology of events involving both the evolution of these cases and the implementation process of the initiative. Based on this chronology, a summary for each project was constructed to study the behavior of all relevant stakeholders, including the identification of their respective objectives and use of resources, and the project's outcome. These summaries were then used to determine the outcomes of projects and the specific management strategies used by key actors as identified in Table 8. After their identification, the specific management strategies were classified according to categories of vertical activities or horizontal activities (Agranoff & McGuire, 2003).

According to their classification, these strategies were used to evaluate each stakeholder to improve conditions for the completion of the cultural district's shared goals and the extent to which the decision making process reflects democratic ideals. These outcomes were evaluated according to five favorable interaction, protecting the quality and transparency of interactions, and exercising prudent use of network structuring (Agranoff & McGuire 2001; Kickert et al., 1997; Klijn et al., 1995). Indicators for the five criteria are found in Table 9.

Table 8 Management Activities

Vertical Activities	Horizontal Activities
Seeking general program information	Gaining policy making assistance
Seeking new funding of programs and projects	Engaging in formal partnerships
Seeking interpretation of standards and rules	Engaging in joint policy making and strategy – making
Seeking general program guidance	Consolidating policy effort
Regulatory Relief, flexibility or waiver	Seeking financial resources
Statutory relief or flexibility	Contracting for planning and implementation
Request Change in Official Policy	Establishing a partnership for the project
Seeking funding innovation of existing program	Seeking technical assistance
Requesting model program involvement	
Requesting performance – based discretion	

Source: Adapted from Agranoff & McGuire (2003).

Table 9 Evaluation Criteria

Criteria	Indicators
Activation of Members	Type of actors secured by government and the level of resources they committed to the network; identifying which actors were able to achieve their own objectives with limited costs
Securing Commitment	Type of agreement (such as informal agreement or formal contract) secured from these actors
Synthesizing Conditions for Favorable Interaction	Type and frequency of use of game management strategies (such as promoting the exchange of information, facilitating interaction, and establishing rules, using incentives)
Prudent Use of Network Structuring	Type and frequency of use of network structuring strategies (such as changing the relations between actors, changing established rules, and altering the distribution of resources)
Quality and Transparency of Interaction	Type of meetings (public or private) and attendees that were conducted to direct the implementation of the cultural district initiative; dissemination of information to the public

Source: Adapted from Kickert et al. (1997); Klijn et al. (1995).

基于重要性和表现维度的中国创意文化产业区分析

5. Three Successful Cases of Cultural District

5.1 Avenue of the Arts in Philadelphia of America

Following World War Two, Philadelphia, like many northeastern and northern central cities, struggled with a decreasing tax base as both its employment and populations migrated to the suburbs. As Clark, Jr. & Clark (1982) note, Philadelphia and its suburbs from 1946 to 1970 symbolized the problems confronting cities: Population shifts, changing technology, and social transformation. By this time, Philadelphia's downtown development was no longer driven by growth and industrialization, instead, it was now marked by the absence of growth (Adams et al., 1991). The city's downtown infrastructure had become obsolete due to the lack of investment since the 1920's. By the late 1940s, Philadelphia had became a "worn-out city" with sixty percent of its industrial buildings outdated and 30000 properties vacant (Adde, 1969). The quality of Philadelphia's housing stock was also quite poor (Clark, Jr. & Clark, 1982). Roughly half of the city's housing had been constructed in the nineteenth century. Given its age, the housing was deteriorating. Overcrowding, neglect, and illegal subdivisions were also negative factors that undermined good housing stock and discouraged investment. Therefore, new suburban housing had a strong appeal. While Philadelphia's population declined, its suburbs grew rapidly. From 1950 to 1970, the suburban percentage of the SMSA (Standard Metropolitan Statistical Area) for Philadelphia increased from 30% to 52% (U.S. Census Bureau 1952, 1972). In this same period, the percentage of blacks in Philadelphia rose from 18% to 34% (U.S. Census Bureau, 1972, 1952).

Despite the city's economic troubles, the arts in Philadelphia flourished ad cultural and educational institutions expanded in the 1950s and 1960s (Clark, Jr. & Clark, 1982). The Philadelphia Museum of Art continued to grow with the support of the city and gifts from the city's elite. The Pennsylvania Academy of the Fine Arts opened a second building, the Peale House on Chestnut Street in 1964. In 1966, the Library Company of Philadelphia move from the Ridgway Library on South Broad Street to a modern facility on Locust Street next to the Historical Society of Philadelphia. The Free

Library of Philadelphia rapidly expanded by doubling its stock of books. The Academy of Music was also restored and designated a National Historical Landmark in 1963. Due to the post war's population boom and the G. I. Bill, Philadelphia's institutions of higher learning experienced tremendous growth (Clark, Jr. & Clark, 1982). In the 1960s, the University of Pennsylvania and Drexel University moved forward with a joint redevelopment plan named University City (Carlson 1999; Meyerson et al., 1978). The plan called for the construction of new teaching and science facilities as well as dormitories. Proposed facilities included a new building for Penn's Wharton School, a Physics Department Laboratory, and a multi-building science center. To support the plan, the Philadelphia Planning Commission certified and area in West Philadelphia south of Market Street for redevelopment in 1948. It was worth of mentioning here is during the age of Rendell administration, he made a growth plan of redeveloping local economy by continuing to project Avenue of art Philadelphia. At that time, Rendell was also with additional job losses as remaining manufacturers continued to close or leave the city. For example, the U. S. Navy decided to finally close its shipyard in South Philadelphia. Rendell attempted attract the German shipbuilding firm Meyer Werft to use the location as a production facility, which would provide over 6000 manufacturing jobs. However, Pennsylvania's Republican governor, Tom Ridge, demanded that the company contribute more of its own capital to the venture rather than depending mainly on public investment. As a result, Meyer Werf withdrew from the plan. Recognizing the manufacturing sector would not return to its former strength, Rendell adopted a service sector base economic development strategy. Drawing on completion of the $500 million convention center in 1993, he sought projects that would continue to revitalize Philadelphia's downtown and increase tourism by capitalizing on Philadelphia's cultural and entertainment attractions (Bissigner, 1997). His downtown development projects involved the construction of hotels, apartments, and retail. Large initiatives included the Avenue of the Arts cultural district, the rebuilding of Independence Mall, and the redevelopment of the Naval Shipyard.

The Avenue of the Arts initiative provided Rendell with a possible means for marketing the city's cultural assets while staving off South Broad Street's continued decline. Despite its decline, South Broad Street has several important cultural attractions. The Academy of Music was still in use and had become the oldest operating grand opera house in the United States. Considered one of Philadelphia's cultural treasures, its opulent interior still drew audiences. The Academy of Music and its major resident companies, the Philadelphia Orchestra, the Pennsylvania Ballet, and the Opera Company of Philadelphia were considered to be attractions for the district's development. The University of the Arts was now located on South Broad Street. The University of the Arts has also renovated the deteriorating Schubert Theater into the Merriam Theater. In addition, the Pennsylvania Ballet had purchased a building for teaching and rehearsal space further South at Broad and Washington Streets. Based on these factors, momentum began to grow for developing South Broad Street into the Avenue of the Arts, a performing arts cultural district. Given these emerging projects, the Avenue of the Arts initiative promised the possibility of restring both Philadelphia and South Broad Street to its former glory, which had become a "symbolic boulevard of broken dreams" (Lemann, 2000).

With initiatives like the Avenue of the Arts, Rendell's economic development plan focused on reinventing Philadelphia's image as a "second city" that was an important destination for investment and tourism (Hodos, 2002). By promoting the city's historical and cultural assets of Philadelphia, Rendell boosted both the revenue and morale of the city. While Rendell could not return Philadelphia to its former economic strength, at the end of his two terms, he was successful in making some economic gains. In addition to revenue – generating the Avenue of the Arts.

5.2 Insa – Dong Cultural District of South Korea

Insa – Dong is not only a real name of place but also represents traditional culture street. Through reviewing the history and its developing track, the study found that there are 5 areas and 52 Fangs, 775 Dongs. "Insa – Dong" originated from the bigger area of "KuanRen Fang" and smaller area of "Big Insa – Dong", and pick up one word from both of the name of area to form the name of Insa – Dong. In Korean era, Seoul has set up an organization which was called "Han Government Office". The Government Office administrated the city of Seoul according to the mentioned criterion of city formation in the "Zhou Li" that provided a standard for city planning. At that time, the geography of Seoul city is not totally suitable for the criterion, therefore, it only was used to the planning of other facilities, and Insa – Dong just located in the middle of "Kuan Ren Fang". At the end of Korea era, some rich man bought land and build houses to enlarge their own land. The demand of house has been increased with the increasing of population and lead to appear many big houses, and land at the two sides of the street.

Chapter Two Literature Review

After the end of Korean, Insa – Dong increasingly has been become today's Insa – Dong street because of administration organization's settling down in the area. Insa – Dong rapidly became a central market for exchange of antiques, while Korean government has been forced to sign the "Yiwei treaty" in 1905. Business man began to engage in antiques and traditional artworks for rich man in the village where those scholar – officials of Korean era live, then Insa – Dong street has been formed originally. During Japan colony era in last century 1920s, lots of business man began to pack into Insa – Dong because the business district where Japanese live has developed in Ming – Dong and Zhongwu – Dong. On the other side, the languished scholar – officials of previous dynasty sold their antiques in this market, antiques dealers got together here and some antiques shops have emerged for those Japanese who were fun of collecting antiques. With more and more antiques shops emerged in Insa – Dong, some small book shops also were opened around the Insa – Dong. Moreover, more and more people such as artists, painters and antiques buyers come to Insa – Dong, some tea – houses and restaurants served for these people also emerged, and Insa – Dong business district has been formed increasingly. At the end of Japan colony era, lots of scholar – official's land were divided to small piece of land because their family declined, and finally it formed today's formation of street.

In 1988, Insa – Dong was appointed to be "Traditional Cultural Street" and regarded by people as a "Traditional Street". Finally, Insa – Dong was appointed to be the first cultural district and set up management systems by government in 2003 until now days. Basing on two reasons that Insa – Dong was appointed to be cultural district, firstly, Insa – Dong assembled lots of galleries, art works and ancient arts and facilities related to arts; secondly, it still keeps the construction and old buildings style of Korea, in the atmosphere of traditional space people can feel the happiness and savor. The transition of Insa – Dong could be summarized as table 10:

Table 10 The Transition of Insa – Dong Cultural District

Era	Events		Results and Influence	
Beginning of Korea	Resource accumulation	Scholar – official residence	Artists crowded together	Entertainment place for scholar – official
Middle of Korea			Population flow	Land divided

continued table

Era	Events		Results and Influence	
End of Korea			Scholar – official residence	
Japan colony	Resource outflow	Decline of scholar – official	Many antiques outflow	Antiques place for Japanese
Liberation		Japanese retreat	Japanese sold antiques	Local people's antiques market
1960s	Traditional commercial diffusion	Antiques prosperous	Shops related to arts move in	
1970s			Foreigner travelling	Mery's Alley
1980s			Favorable policies	Appointed to be traditional cultural street
1990s	Traditional culture tourism	Policy making and development	Appointed to be "street of car clearance"	More travelers and investment
2000s			Appointed to be cultural district	Culture commercialization

In order to achieve management of Insa – Dong cultural district, the Government of Jongno – Gu has drafted a "management planning of Insa – Dong cultural district" which was approved by Seoul mayor. The plan includes the following several aspects that encourage the support of facilities, cultural space creation, activities' planning and establishment of residential association. In order to achieve a more efficient results in the cultural district management. Management of the Insa – Dong guidance was divided to several levels as table 11:

Table 11 Operational Guidance for Cultural District Management Plane

Classification	Support and control matters	Content
Encourages facilities Support plan	Tax exemption	The registration tax, property tax and city planning tax 50% reduction
	Financial support	New, alterations, the construction of facilities for the costs of operating cost, Identity Assurance Support Limited won 5000
	In support	Encourages the support facilities

Chapter Two Literature Review

continued table

Classification	Support and control matters	Content
Cultural space construction and management plan	Industrial limitation	Unit plans of the industry in the cultural area of the specified limit' after the comprehensive use restriction and center street use restriction
	Use change limit	Use the change is needed to examine the suitability of the purpose, meets the requirements
	Outdoor advertisement	The Center and the periphery street outside the house advertising placement and color limitations
Program and activities support planning	The selection of traditional expertise	Meet a certain standard for business premises designated as traditional expertise and provide help
	Activities support	Support the activities organized by the inhabitants of the Council, but prohibit activity of pure entertainment
Residents agreement and support planning	Construction of residents agreement	Insa – Dong traditional cultural preservation of the Center for which constitute the hold regular meetings
	Support of resident agreement	Financial support for operation

Certainly, the phenomenon of commercialization Insa – Dong is more serious that can affect the traditional cultural district as a symbolization of Korea. Because worrying about over commercialization of Insa – Dong, Insa – Dong was appointed to be cultural district by Seoul city government. From then on, the ratio of common industry has been decreasing from 74.7 percent to around 65.4 percent in 2005. It is obvious, although Insa – Dong cultural districts was designated and managed in a range with good results, however, for cultural district prior to specified business premises already exists in the common industry, it is still hard to achieve effective control and over more than half of the industry is still common industry in Insa – Dong cultural district. Therefore, Insa – Dong looks more like a purchasing and food street than a traditional cultural art street on the view of both sides of the street, but more ironic is the fact that it is precisely for this reason that Insa – Dong attracted a large number of tourists from domestic and aboard. However, if Insa – Dong cultural district lost traditional culture position, it will not only damage the art function but also commercial value. Basing on this reason, the people engage in the common industrial also care about management and fostering of Insa – dong cultural district.

基于重要性和表现维度的中国创意文化产业区分析

After experiencing the above – mentioned rough and visible changes in Insa – Dong, the cultural district is still named as "Korean traditional culture street", the main reason is that different cities compete for the limited space of the resources and they need to emphasize and out – stand its own charm and characteristics. Therefore, Insa – Dong cultural district has become a symbolization of expressing city's own characteristics should be used effectively in the wave of commercialization. For this point, not only foreign tourists and dealers in various industrial of Insa – Dong cultural district but also a token of outstanding local cultural and art figures at national level have a unprecedented identical. Actually, it is not only this kind of thing happened in Insa – Dong, but also in 798 cultural district, therefore, the study will present and analyze 798 cultural district to show some truth between two cultural districts and try to find some interesting facts.

5.3 Seven – Nine – Eight Cultural District in China

The Establishment of 798 Factory

Beijing 798 Art District in the location of beginning establishment of China, the first Five – Year Plan for building the Beijing North China United Radio Equipment Factory which were called 718 joint factories. 718 joint factories is personally approved by Premier Zhou Enlai and Prime Minister, the Minister WANG ZHENG command planning. The former Soviet Union and democratic German participated in aiding to build. In 1952, the joint factory in the suburbs of Beijing Industrial Base without Wine Immortal Bridge the planning of the 1954 start construction in October 1957. Construction of national leadership involved in the groundbreaking ceremony for the construction of production in Wine Immortal Bridge areas and 718 joint factory. At the same time, the two plants construction of 774 and 738 factories changed not only the Wine Immortal Bridge area but also the situations of China electronics industry, they have developed on the history of the beginning of the great development. 718 joint has made excellent contribution to electronics industry and communications industry after the completion.

Formation, Development and Rising

In December 2000, the Original 700 Factory, 706 Factory, 707 Plant, 718 Plant, 797 Plant and 798 Factory became to the reorganization of consolidation, Beijing Electronic Science and technology group Co., Ltd. Seven Star Group is one of the Beijing Municipality and Electronic City Park first verified high and new technology enterprise which owe to the original factory assets have been re – consolidation a part of the premises have been idle. In order to make this part of the premises to be fully exploited, these plants have been continuously carried out for renting by seven star group Co. , Ltd. In February 2002, the Americans, Robert rented 120 square meters canteens, it caused a Muslim shop in front of the recurrent and have fellowship with him were also successively here who had the luxury of space and the cheap rent. Because some of the plant is a classic modernism package, they have Bauhaus architectural style, therefore, it attracted many artists who came to settle and increasingly emerged today's 798 cultural & art district.

Figure 3 Bauhaus Architectraual Style Building

From 2001, the local perimeter artist and outside of Beijing artists began to gather in 798 factories area, they found here by an artist and unique vision to engage in artistic work to became unique advantages. Make full use of their original factory style (Germany Package Moorhouse architectural style), decorated and furnished to become a characteristic of the arts and creative space. There were nearly 200 companies involved in the arts and cultural institutions into this area. According to the March 2005 incomplete statistics, 798 Art District mainly includes the creation and exchange of class two major categories, most of them are belong to the artistic creation, space design, advertising design, home furniture design and fashion and Image Design. At least 300 more artists living in 798 Art District as their main artistic creation, as well as from abroad such as artists of France, the United States, Belgium, the Netherlands, Australia, South Korea, Singapore, and so on. Some celebrated artist like Liu Suola (Screenplay, music), Hong huang (people, publishing house), Li ZongSheng (music) and Lee Sang – chun (Sculptor) also have a nameless anonymous.

Artists and their companies hire space of 798 Art District, from several thousand square meters to a few dozen square meters in size. Of these, some large art institutions and companies have established workshop in 798 cultural district such as a Belgium art companies (rented space art 4500 square meters) and southern California Institute of Architects (rented space more than 4000 square meters), followed by LI XIA leased in the space exhibition galleries and (2000 square meters), magazines such as the rented space (1610 square meters), Kim Sung (1350 square meters). The world – famous Guggenheim Art Company intends to hire the 798 Art District in 5000 to 10000 m venues of the Arts District, but it has no so large areas of the places where you can rent. As a result of the "Heap artist" effect and celebrity effect, it has undertaken a two session Beijing Dashanzi International Arts Festival since 2004. The artistic district of 798 is growing influence on. The inaugural Festival (2004 April – May one month) attracted 80000 people to come and visit, with about 60 percent of the Chinese audience and 40 per cent for overseas visitors, of which there are from Paris in major cities such as the representative of the contemporary art. More than 120 Chinese and foreign media reported the Arts Festival and their art works. Some of the domestic and international cultural institutions and foundations of the festival provided sponsors. The second session of the Festival (2005 April 30 to 22 March), 23 days, conducted a total of performances, display, studies artistic activities, attract audiences 109 million or more, up to 80000 a day of nearly a million people. September 22 to October 7, 798 Arts District conducted the "biennale", also the fruitful outcome of the audience, the audience close to 6 million. More than a few large activities to make the 798 Art District increase popularity of art trading volume.

Since 2004, the Prime Minister of Sweden and Switzerland, the Prime Minister, the German Chancellor Gerhard Schroeder (Austria), the Prime Minister, the President of the European Union (Barroso), Belgium, princess, Mrs. Nane Annan, French President Chirac, have one after another have visited the 798 Art District. Schroeder visited 798 Art District Exclamation: A few decades ago, building of Bauhaus style architect in Germany was seldom found but today could be seen in Beijing, it's really phenomenal! Belgium Princess spent a few million dollars to buy art works.

In 2003 the United States Arts District 798 Time magazine as one of the most emblematic of the cultural 22 city art centers. In the same year, Beijing for the first time elected to Newsweek annual 12 large cities in the world, because of the 798 Art District a waste into a stylish communities 65387640. In 2004, Beijing was included in the United States on the Fortune Magazine annual award of the world development in 20 cities, selected rationale remains as 798. Over the past two to three years, more and more people come to visit the 798 Art District for purchasing art works. According to a survey conducted in 2004, about 45 million people access to 798 cultural district and the overseas visitors and domestic visitors by approximately 4 : 6.

Figure 4　The History of 798 Cultural District

Positioning

After moving into 798 cultural district, Artists and cultural institutions greatly rent and transform the vacant factories into a gallery, arts center, artist studios, design company and dining bar and became the aggregation in the form of a "SOHO color to the internationalization of the art of agglomeration" and "lifestyle", causing a considerable degree of concern. Through combination of contemporary art, floor space and cultural industries and history of a pulse and the organic integration of the urban living environment, 798 cultural district has evolved into a cultural concepts, it generated a strong appeal for the various types of professionals and the general public and great effectiveness on urban culture and the concept of survival space. Great in – situ architecture and bright sunroof are rare, they were built by the former Soviet Union in the early 1950s. Accompanied by reform and opening up as well as the Beijing urban culture positioning and transformation of life style and the wave of globalization, 798 factories are facing up a further redevelopment tasks. As urbanization process and the expansion of the urban area, former members of the big mountain, on the outskirts of the sub – region has now become a part of the town, the existing industrial relocation, inevitably rise on the site of the city is more suitable for positioning and development trends, pollution – free, low power consumption and high – tech industries. A large number of artists moved into culture district, which is reaction of the historical trend.

This group included design, publication, display, performances and cultural industries such as artist studios, it also included boutique home, fashion, bars, restaurants and cakes in the service industry. In the historical and cultural legacies to protecting the premise, they take the creative understanding for design and transformation of the architecture and lifestyle. After these vacant factories were transformed by these artists became a new construction. It developed an interesting dialog between historical clue and development paradigm, utility and aesthetic.

This group of persons in ways of surviving itself is a product of economic reform, they show a personal concept and the socioeconomic fabric of the new relationship between Utopia and reality – in the memory and the future. In the new period of the 798 youth culture through the accumulation of carrier. This culture would be the internationalization of local resources, is the ideal personal socialization. The new 798 means that the vanguard and traditional style coexistence of awareness of the experiment with social responsibility and color, spiritual pursuit and economic planning win – win, and the mass of the elite interaction. This phenomenon of 798 cultural districts is involved in urban development for production and consumption.

Events of Development

The 798 Art District real access to people of vision, principally from the beginning of the year 2002, of which an important events such as the developments in Xu Yong – space establishment, Tokyo in Gallery and the subsequent "recycling" activities such as the 798 Prior to that, although the space has already begun a succession of being rental, use, for example the Central Academy of Fine Arts rental of space here so classrooms, the magazine in Hong, but this is not strictly a 798 Art District Period. Because 798 in 2002, both before and after the phase, there is a relatively large difference in 2002 prior to the move in, to a certain degree, is simply the tenants, with seven star group is the relationship between the simple tenancy relationships. In 2002 after the actors, such as Xu Yong, Wong Yui et al. and the development of an attempt to build the 798, makes it a Chinese contemporary art zone, so in a strict sense, since that time, the transformation of the 798 action artists become a conscious action of the transformation of the region features, 798 had only just begun in a real sense. The 798 Art District in the face of some of the major events in the comb attachment, with a view to the adoption of its function to restore episode of recycling process. The following table is summary of events for development (In the year 2002 as the starting point, the region features 798 recycling divided into two periods before, it is not in the strict sense of the Arts District has been stage, but part of the artist, thus transforming from a functional perspective, this period can be seen as the preparation

Chapter Two Literature Review

period of the Art Deco District, or known as the pan 798 Art District period).

Table 12　Events of Development in 798 Cultural Districts

Time	Events	Persons, organizations	Remarks
Before years of 2000	Some organizations settled down	The Central Academy of Fine Arts Department of Sculpture, magazine, as well as minority artist	During this period had no effect on basic
2000	Enter the artists and the early institutions	Sui jianguo, Hong Huang	The Central Academy of Fine Arts Department of Sculpture after removal, Sui Mingtai of statehood will own studio set in the 798 factory in a kiln shop. The famous publisher of the Hong and homes in the aftermath of moving to 798 factory
2001		Liu suola (after then, some artists like Huang rui, Cang xin, Bai yiluo, and Chen lingyang moved in one after another)	Vanguard of the famous musicians who the writer Liu Sola together with your own music moved into 798 factory
2002		Robert	In June 2002, the Americans enter 798 Art District Robert Mugabe, the establishment of the "eight arts Time Zone", start-up bookstores. It is now the site of the original 798 by Muslim converted canteens
2002. 10	The Tokyo Art Works (also known as the Tokyo Art galleries) emplacement 798, and made the "Beijing First Ukiyoe" ①		The event received social and artistic community concerns, is the Art Deco District, the first major event of child care, from 798 Art District real access to people of vision

---

① The exhibition for the importance of the 798 Art District, Shu Yang in the 798 Art District in the past and present, for the record: "Mr Beijing Ukiyoe, 'with more domestic and foreign institutions and artists and arts in the areas of the Arts District 798, 798 the size of the initial presentation. It can be said that Beijing Ukiyoe', is the opening of the 798 Art District started the first landmark event."

continued table

Time	Events	Persons, organizations	Remarks
At the end of 2002	The completion of the transformation of the space-time	Xu yong	Xu Yong had been planning the "Hutong tour", thereby precipitating a culture of Houhai
2003	Recycling 798	Huang rui, Xu yong	In the month of April 2003 the recycling activities, 798 had provided 798 Art District Function Transformation, also stepped up its planning themselves after breaking the original vegetation in the arts district substantially speed, 798 cultural district has been formed
2003.4	Initial shape of the Arts District		Include galleries, art Foundation, published media advertising, design, fashion brand, Coffee Shop, Restaurant, Bar, approximately 38 organizations and 46 artist studios
	For the first time in Beijing in 2003 Elected to the original United States "News week" selection of the annual world cities		The reason is that the exists of 798 artistic district. The Publication View, 798 Arts District the existence and development of Beijing, as the capital of the world and future potential of the capacity
2004.4-5	First Beijing Dashanzi Art Festival	Organizer: Huang rui, Xu yong et al. Participating Institutions: The centennial impression that Lu Shisheng cultural dissemination center for the arts, Beijing season	The 798 Art District was finally established, in fact benefit from Dashanzi Art Festival, if no dashanzi technology, may not have the 798 Art District. In addition, this festival is a civilian forces represented by the institutions of civil society in the creation of large-scale international contemporary arts activities
2005	Bauhaus architectural style in 798 Art District, taken by the Beijing municipal government building as "Excellent modern buildings"		798 Art District building from the fate of the inevitability of the Arts District has been allowed to continue exist

Chapter Two Literature Review

continued table

Time	Events	Persons, organizations	Remarks
2006	The 798 Art District are listed with the first batch of cultural and creative cultural industries		
2006.3	Construction Administrative Office of 798 cultural district was established		The Government of the Chaoyang District, Beijing, Seven Star Group established a leading group for the 798 Art District and has 798 Art District Building Management Office, to the coordination, Services, boot, management as the purpose of advancing the art deco district cultural industrial development
2007.4	Art Festival of 798 cultural district Beijing 2007	Cultural district administrative office	The main theme of peace after the 70 "affordable", 14 art days, attracted global tourists visiting

The operation and management system of 798 Cultural District:

The 798 Cultural District has different level for operation and management system which the interdependence between elements of the Internet as a prerequisite. Its main components include: Artists, district managers, enter the park area of community groups outside of the operating agencies such as other art galleries, institutions and other bodies such as the business. These different components through the market together, forming a complete arts management system, poses a complex multi-interactive chain.

The primary operation and management level is called main system. It is Cultural District internal functioning of the system. It can be seen as a closed system, from this point of view, it is a form of self-sufficiency system, its own internal dimensions of the forged between a symbiotic relationships. The following diagram shows the relationship:

From above diagram we can see that there are two main levels, production and circulation. It is that to say the artists of the production and the production of artists around the art market, which is the circulation chain. In this chain of artists and art gallery is a one-to-from the core relationship. The 798 Art District in the early stages of the artist in the structure of the Center, other ingredients is all around the artist. In this regard, the process of inspection of 798 cultural district, most of the respondents considered that the artists should be at the heart of the campus, because in the 798 Art District in the initial stage of artists in the 798 Art District and the popularity of this have the substantial in, there were also different forces to divide. When the rents soaring in the constant enhancement of the tendency to commercialization, artists began to evacuate 798 Art District Action. Thus become a new artistic district of galleries and the force at the core of the Arts District started the 798 a artists area into a gallery of the congregation, while artists at the park's status beginning slowly to marginalization, but artists as well as the life of an artist status is still our connection with 798 Art District together.

The secondary system can be illustrated as following:

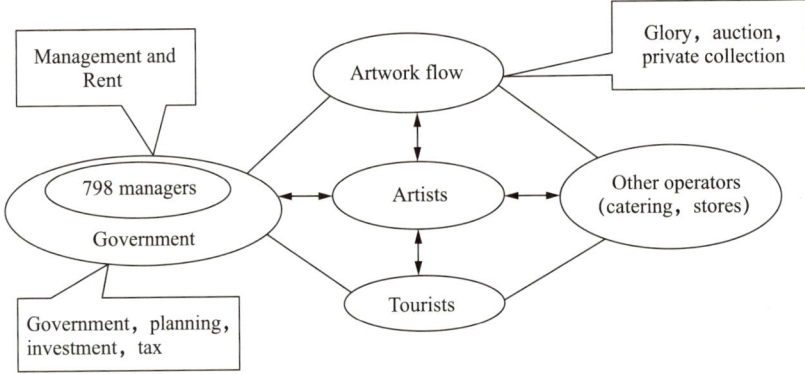

Diagram 3   The Main System of Interactive Management System 798 Cultural District

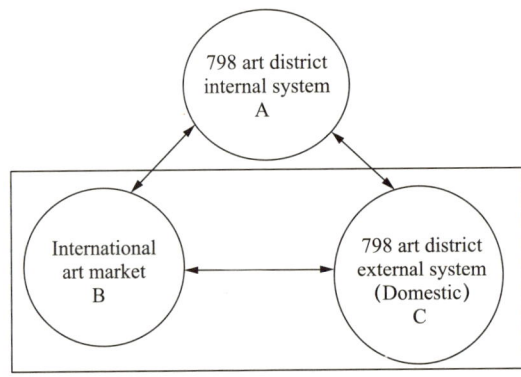

Diagram 4   Illustration of 798 Cultural District Interactive Secondary System

The system is in the black box, B and C respectively represent the artistic district

Chapter Two Literature Review

of external systems is the art of the diversity and openness, from the Art District and internal system exchange, they are in the same level and both of them have diversified and interactive relationship with the 798 Art District. The arts community on the one hand rendering self – sufficiency and the status of the self – improvement, while with the international and domestic art market relations have a close exchanges, both for international and domestic art market as well as gradually gaining market recognition of and access to the art of the process. If we say that the Yuanmingyuan Artist Village Period Dialog language and contemporary art of the legitimacy of the struggle for is still in its initial stages in the bud, that is in a "underground", "semi – underground" state, then the 798 Art District period is complete from the "underground", half the "underground" status to the ground status changes, as a result of today's international and domestic markets for the contemporary arts is hot, making the contemporary art creation and operation of the public view, art markets to promote contemporary arts and arts in the development of communities has played a great role. In campus external system, particularly in the context of a global culture of the international art market interaction, both external forces on the impact of the campus, while at the campus of the impact of the external system. This role is a two – way interactive relationships, impact can be either positive or negative. Their complexity hidden deep in the internal forces, rivalry and gaming makes it possible for various complex relations, it involves not only the artistic district of its problems, but also to the political, economic, cultural, ideological and artistic communities at the state of survival realistic issues. The international art market is from the development of art begun earlier in the spectrum of contemporary art in the experiment has not been recognized by the cultural mainstream institutions and of contemporary art in Western art market recognition. At that time the most active art critic Li xianting of the earliest caused the attention of Europeans and because his family life in Beijing, so for many artists are very important and Li xianting also have many artists opens the door and the growth of these artists and recommending played an important role. If the interaction with the international market more to make China's contemporary arts accredited, then with 798 external system such as social public, media and other interactive allow 798 Art District become a concern of the Community Arts, Art Zone development and protection would gradually gain social and Government, thus at the policy level for the survival of the space. Through the 798 Art District Internal interactive system and external interactions system analysis, it can be seen that the various elements of the diversified and interactive, constitutes a unique cultural district management mechanism.

Chapter Three   Analysis of Cultural District in China

1. Importance—performance Analysis

1.1 Concept of Importance—Performance Analysis

This is an easily – applied technique for measuring attribute importance and performance can further the development of effective marketing programs. Firms conducting attribute research to measure consumer acceptance of particular features of their marketing programs frequently encounter problems in translating the results into action. Several factors may contribute to his situation, but two are particularly troublesome:

Management may find it difficult to understand the practical significance of research findings expressed in term of "coefficients of determination" and "level of stress" . The research may have examined only one side of the consumer acceptance question – either attribute importance of attribute performance rather than both.

Yet empirical research has demonstrated that consumer satisfaction is a function of both expectations related to certain important attributes and judgments of attribute performance. In light of these considerations, importance – performance analysis has been found to be a useful technique for evaluating the elements of a marketing program. The technique draws on conceptual contributions to be found in many places in the literature. A specific example offered here will highlight the approachto present a case where the technique was clearly useful.

1.2 An Application of Important—Performance Measurement Tool

An automobile dealer's service records indicated that only 37% of its new car buyers remained loyal service customers after the 6000 mile service. The firm hoped to increase that figure to 50% as a means of improving service department profits as well as

Chapter Three Analysis of Cultural District in China

stimulating repeat sales of new vehicles. A literature search and conversations with service and sales department personnel and factory representatives identified 14 attributes which were felt to affect service department patronage. Respondent were then asked two questions about each attribute: How important is this feature? How well did the dealer perform? Questionnaires were mailed to customers who had purchased a new car from the dealer between one and two years earlier. An attractive feature of importance – performance analysis is that the results may be graphically displayed on an easily – interpreted, two – dimensional grid. The 28 attribute ratings from Exhibit 1 are plotted as 14 points on the importance – performance grid in Exhibit 1. The numbers refer to the attributes listed in Exhibit 2. The labels of the quadrants A, B, C & D refer to marketing effort. For example, "Concentrate Here" denotes an area (A) where attributes are important and also where performance can be improved. Concentrating constructive action in this area would produce maximum results.

Table 13 Importance and Performance Ratings for
Automobile Dealer's Service Development

Attribute Number	Attribute Description	Mean Importance Rating[a]	Mean Performance Rating[b]
1	Job done right the first time	3.83	2.63
2	Fast action on complaints	3.63	2.73
3	Prompt warranty work	3.60	3.15
4	Able to do any job needed	3.56	3.00
5	Service available when needed	3.41	3.05
6	Courteous and friendly service	3.41	3.29
7	Car ready when promised	3.38	3.03
8	Perform only necessary work	3.37	3.11
9	Low prices on service	3.29	2.00
10	Clean up after service work	3.27	3.02
11	Convenient to home	2.52	2.25
12	Convenient to work	2.43	2.49
13	Courtesy buses and rental cars	2.37	2.35
14	Send out maintenance notices	2.05	3.33

a: Ratings obtained from a four – point scale of "extremely important" "important" "slightly important" and "not important".

b: Ratings obtained from a four – point scale of "excellent" "good" "fair" and "poor".

Source: Martilla JA and James JC, 1977.

Above table could be illustrated by charter as follow:

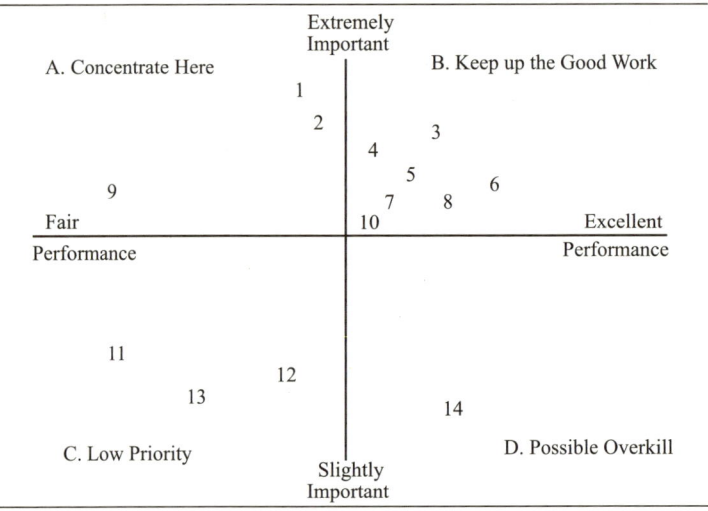

Diagram 5   Importance – Performance Grid with Attribute Ratings for Automobile Dealer's Service Department

Management Application: Interpretation of the importance – performance grid may be illustrated with examples taken from each of the four quadrants.

A. Concentrate here. Customers feel that low service prices (Attribute 9) are very important but indicate low satisfaction with the dealer's performance.

B. Keep up with the good work. Customers value courteous and friendly service (Attribute 6) and are pleased with the dealer's performance.

C. Low priority. The dealer is rated low in terms of providing courtesy buses and rental cars (Attribute 13), but customers do not perceive this feature to be very important.

D. Possible overkill. The dealer is judged to be doing a good job of sending out maintenance notices (Attribute 14), but customers attach only slight importance to them (However, there may be other good reasons for continuing this practice).

Developing Marketing Strategies: Importance – performance analysis provides management with a useful focus for developing marketing strategies. In the case of service prices, for example, at least there strategies or combinations of strategies might be considered:

Firstly, the dealer could meet the price issue head – on through informative advertising showing that the dealer's rates are lower than service station prices or by running coupon specials for service work performed back periods of the week.

Secondly, given the high importance attached to doing the job right the first time

(Attribute 1) and fast action on complaints (Attribute 2), the dealer might attempt to make customers feel that his service rates are worth paying by improving his performed during slack periods of the week.

Thirdly, the dealer might lessen the impact of his perceived high service prices by selling customers an extended warranty which would reduce out – of – pocket repair charges and encourage their returning to the dealer for regular maintenance.

Tips on using importance – performance analysis: The first is to determining what attributes to measure is critical, for if evaluative factors important to the customers are overlooked, the usefulness of importance – performance analysis will be severely limited. Development of the attribute list should begin with identifying key features of the marketing mix. Previous research in the same or related areas, various qualitative research techniques, such as focus groups and unstructured personal interviews and managerial judgment, all are useful in identifying potentially important factors which might otherwise be missed. These sources can also provide guidance for screening the attribute list down to a manageable size in order to avoid low response rates and unnecessary data manipulation; The second is to separate the importance measures and the performance measures helps to minimize compounding and order effects. If the respondent were asked in one question about the importance of price and in the next question about his satisfaction with current price levels, his answer to the first may influence his response to the second. By grouping all of the importance measures in one section and all of the performance measures in a later section, the respondent moves in a natural progression from general to more specific questions with a distinct separation between his ratings for each attribute; The third is positioning the vertical and horizontal axes on the grid is a matter of judgment. The value of this approach lies in identifying relative, rather than absolute, levels of importance and performance. Frequently a five or seven – point scale will yield a good spread of ratings, and the middle position will constitute a useful division for the grid. Occasionally, as in the above example, the absence of low importance and performance ratings may argue for moving the axes over one position on the scale; The fourth is median values as a measure of central tendency are theoretically preferable to means because a true interval scale ma not exist. However, the investigator may wish to compute both values and, if the two consistently appear reasonably close, use the means to avoid discarding the additional information they contain. Since tests of significance are not being used, distortions introduced by minor violations of the interval – scale assumption are unlikely to be serious; The fifth is to analyze the importance – performance grid, it is systematically accomplished by considering each attribute in order of its relative importance, moving from the top to the bottom of the grid. Particular attention should be given to the extreme observations since they indicate the greatest disparity between importance and performance and may be key indicators of customer dissatisfaction; The sixth is differences between loyal and disloyal customer ratings may reveal important strategy implications as well as provide validity checks. In the above example, both groups rated low service prices as being high in importance and low in performance, so this attribute by itself would not appear to explain differences in dealer patronage. Prompt warranty work, on the other hand, was also rated high in importance by both groups, but loyal service customers rated the dealer's performance considerably higher than the disloyal group. In general, when differences are present between the ratings of loyal and disloyal customer groups, there is greater confidence that the research provides valid attribute measures influencing the buying decision. In summary, importance – performance analysis offers a number of advantages for evaluating consumer acceptance of a marketing program. It is a low – cost, easily understood technique that can yield important insights into which aspect of the marketing mix a firm should devote more attention as well as identify areas that may be consuming too many resources. Presentation of the results on the importance – performance grid facilitates management interpretation of the data and increases their usefulness in making strategic marketing decisions.

2. Empirical Measurement for 798 Cultural District in China by Important – performance

From above analysis for the core successful factors of cultural district in China. Customers has been identified as an important factor to affect the performance and marketing strategies of cultural district, therefore, particularly this study will measure the performance of 798 cultural district to provide strategies for operating cultural district successfully by using importance – performance method.

2.1 Methodology

Data Collection

In order to require the customers of visiting 798 cultural district response, the study designed a self - administered survey questionnaire was used to collect data. The cultural districtattributes were developed by identifying those visitors and management level of cultural district to be adopted as the basis of the items used in this study. Due to differences in cultural, business environment and cultural district operational practices, the items were revised based on Chinese cultural features in order to be more relevant to the Chinese context. A total of 15 attributes was added to the questionnaire and finalized. However, the questionnaire was designed in English and translated into Chinese for survey in 798 cultural district. Two native Chinese scholars with good command of English checked the wording and meaning. To ensure the consistency in translation, the scholars translated the questionnaire again from C hinese to English and compared the results with the original English questionnaire. The structured questionnaire contained two sections. In section one, respondents were asked to rate the perceived importance for each of the 15 cultural district attributes on a 5 - point Likert scale, ranging from "Extremely important" (1) to "Not important" (5). Section two assessed visitors' level of satisfaction with the same attributes on a 5 - point Likert scale ranging from "Very dissatisfied" (1) to "Very satisfied" (5). The sampling framework for the study included all visitors of 798 cultural district. This cultural district fantasy and amusement type of those cultural districts in China and selected for a number of reasons. Firstly, 798 cultural district is in China, contains a unique Chinese elements. It is not a New York, Soho, not on the left bank of France, nor the German Ruhr area, this is China's 798 cultural district. We have seen that the 798 cultural district has various galleries, that of the United States, France, Germany, Belgium, Japan and the DPRK, and it seems like a cultural and arts of the United Nations, but it is not only inclusive, open and generous but also an experimental art area, Chinese culture is an inclusive culture, almost any culture into the soil of China will be able to take root, and has a multi - cultural harmonious development. Secondly, both landscapes and elements from the period following the founding of the PRC, the period of construction of the PRC, the Cultural Revolution of China and the reform and opening up in China. As to Beijing, there are three places must be visited, the great wall, the Forbidden City and the 798 cultural district. The Great Wall, the Forbidden City and Beijing Hutong are presented to the people is traditional and the ancient Beijing, Beijing is the embodiment of this ancient culture. 798 cultural and arts district is a very stylish and very avant - garde, industry and the coexistence of art history and the future, it offers a modern Chinese culture. 798 cultural district is to be seen as the present moment, what is happening is that the development of China. Thirdly, the positioning of 798 cultural district must fall in the arts, since art exist, will form a benign interaction. Many artists find design elements, in addition to Paris, France and Italy Milan Find inspiration and are willing to come to 798 cultural district for inspiration. Here you can see the Forefront of things. It is precisely these avant – garde, Art things that have made 798 cultural district never missing topic. Because of the art of contemporary art, so formed art, design, stylish, media, capital and powers of a benign interaction of the circle. Also because of the arts, 798 cultural district apart from other cultural and creative cultural industries area such as Song Zhuang painting valley etc. Fourthly, original creativity is 798 cultural district's core competitiveness. Creation is the embodiment of life we should attach great importance to intellectual property rights, should be able to accommodate the original, do not easily negate the original. Mere parody might be able to see the benefits of short – term, but no intellectual property rights are limited by the manufacturing industry chain downstream, competitiveness easy to lose. 798 cultural district is China's contemporary art exhibition and trading center in the future will become one of the world's famous art campus, in which show and transactions are taking place in China nowadays, original artwork, this is China's manufacturing to China in the process of creating an indispensable exists.

A convenience sampling approach was used to choose the sample for the study. A self – administered questionnaire was distributed to visitors when visitors waited in restaurants or taking rest in leisure area and then collected immediately after completion. Whoever agreed to participate completed the survey based on his/her personal information. To eliminate any potential bias owing to either group influence or social desirability, it was suggested that the respondents fill out the questionnaire by themselves. If a potential respondent was not willing to participate, then the next convenience sampling unit was chosen. All respondents were assured anonymity. The study will design the questionnaire according to previous similar research of theme park in China, select fifteen questions among fourteen questions and modify them which can be suitable for 798 cultural district (see appendix A).

Data analysis

Data were analyzed via SPSS. Descriptive statistical methods including frequency, mean and Standard Deviation (SD) were used to examine visitors' demographic profiles and measure the levels of importance and satisfaction of 798 cultural district attributes. Paired t-test was applied to test the significant difference between the means of importance and satisfaction. An Importance – Performance Analysis (IPA) was adopted as an analytical framework for this study, where performance was replaced by satisfaction (Rivera et al., 2009; Tonge and Moore, 2007). The IPA has gained popularity among researchers in various disciplines, particularly in measuring the service quality and maintaining high – quality experiences, such as tourism, hospitality, recreation, education, health care and financial institutions (Oh, 2001). In tourism, this technique has been applied to hot spring tourism (Deng, 2007), culinary tourism (Smith and Costello, 2009), tour guide performance (Zhang and Chow, 2004), and a convention center (Breiter and Milman, 2006). The IPA is a procedure that shows respondents' perceptions of the importance of various attributes and the performance of 798 cultural district under study in providing these attributes. Therefore, the importance and performance of the same attributes can be directly compared (Martilla and James, 1997). The results are presented graphically in a two – dimensional matrix as follow illustration:

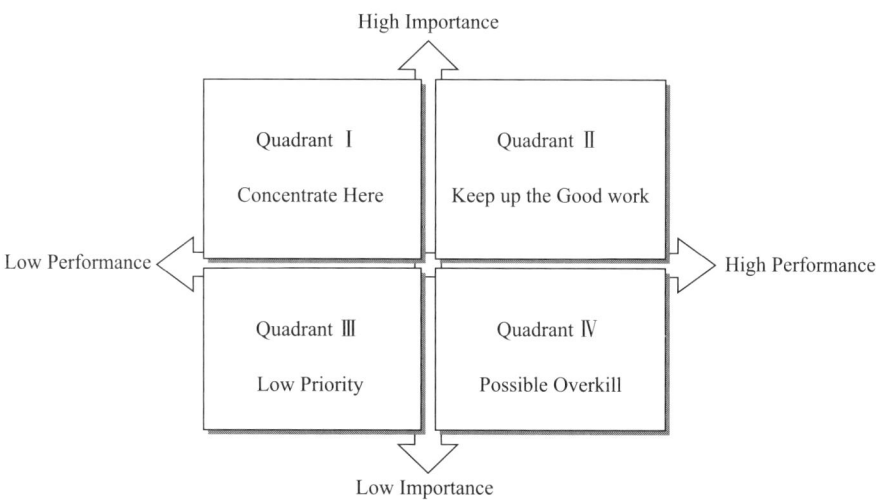

Diagram 6   Importance – performance matrix

Source: Martilla and James (1997).

Moreover, areas for improvements and strategic marketing suggestions can be identified and developed from the visual representation of the results. As shown in diagram 6, attributes in Quadrant I are assessed high in importance and low in performance. This demands immediate attention because a company's performance does not meet the importance level of its products or services. Accordingly, the company needs to "Concentrate Here" on these attributes. Attributes in Quadrant II, evaluated high both in importance and in performance, represent opportunities to maintain and gain competitive advantages. Therefore, the company should "Keep Up the Good Work". Quadrant III includes attributes low both in importance and performance. It is not necessary to focus additional effort here since these attributes are of "Low Priority". Quadrant IV contains attributes rated high in performance but low in importance. It indicates that resources used for these attributes could be better employed in other areas. High performance on unimportant attributes is considered a "Possible Overkill" (Martilla and James, 1977).

Table 14 Demographic Characteristics of the Respondents

Gender (n = 200)	(%)	Age group (years) (n = 200) (%)	Education background (n = 200) (%)	Family status (n = 200) (%)
Female	52.8	18 or under 2.3	Junior or high school 10.6	Single 28.6
Male	47.2	19 – 25 9.4	Vocational school 47.5	Married 71.4
		26 – 35 18.7	Undergraduate 31.7	
		36 – 45 21.2	Master or higher 10.2	
		46 – 55 28.3		
		56 or older 20.1		
Total	100.0	Total 100.0	Total 100.0	Total 100.0

Tonge and Moore (2007) reconceptualized the IPA into an importance – satisfaction approach using satisfaction instead of performance. They argued that comparing importance and satisfaction was more appropriated if the study focused not merely on service provision but also on experience – based visitor outcomes. Rivera et al. (2009) applied the importance – satisfaction analysis to a religious site and

Chapter Three   Analysis of Cultural District in China

concluded that the modified tool provides meaningful implications and additional helpful ideas for the management of religious sites. The context is about case study for Chinese cultural district, where most attributes are strongly experience based. In addition, one of goal for this study is to provide the marketing suggestions for successfully operating cultural district in China. Therefore, this study adopted Tonge and Moore's (2007) approach, replacing performance by satisfaction.

2.2 Results

General profile of the respondents. A total of 200 questionnaires were sent to respondents in the following data collection locations: 100 usable questionnaires were collected in 798 cultural district Beijing. The gender distribution was 52.8% female and 47.2% males. The majority of respondents were married (71.4%) and the rest were single (28.6%). About 10.6% of the respondents completed junior or high school, 12.5% graduated from a vocational school, 48.7% had college education. Most respondents were relatively older than 35 years old. This could be explained the visiting group which are attracted by 798 cultural district, it also reflects the visiting group has more purchasing power for artist works. Table 14 presents the respective level of importance means, level of satisfaction means, gap values, and t – values regarding the differences between importance and satisfaction levels.

Table 15   Levels of Importance and Satisfaction of Perceived Experienced Attributes in Cultural District China

Perceived attributes	Imp mean	Sat mean	T – vale	P – value
Environment and cleanliness of the cultural district	1.63	1.97	10.59	0.000
Map of cultural district for guidance	2.26	2.31	15.07	0.000
Number and quality of arts shows and activities	1.94	2.11	11.19	0.000
Quality of artists' skill in cultural district	2.00	2.14	10.91	0.000
Clear signs for traffic in culture district	2.51	2.57	11.94	0.000
More arts shows and product rather than shops	2.29	2.43	10.43	0.000
Clear open time guidance for exhibition	2.09	2.34	10.31	0.000
Enough parking place in culture district	2.77	2.49	11.94	0.000
Location of cultural district	2.86	1.86	12.69	0.000
Quality of food provided in cultural district	2.06	2.29	12.19	0.000

continued table

Perceived attributes	Imp mean	Sat mean	T-vale	P-value
Number of restaurants	3.40	2.43	20.00	0.000
Layout of the cultural district	2.54	1.97	11.26	0.000
Uniqueness of culture district	1.66	1.77	11.70	0.000
Interactive cultural activities	2.20	2.60	10.18	0.000
Number of automatic selling machine	4.00	3.20	24.39	0.000

The values in Table 14 were sorted in a rank order by the level of importance. The findings indicated that number of automatic selling machine (M = 4.00, SD = 0.97), number of restaurants (M = 3.40, SD = 1.00) were perceived as the most important 2 attributes in 798 cultural district. On the other side, location of cultural district (M = 2.86, SD = 1.33), enough parking place in cultural district (M = 2.77, SD = 1.37), layout of the cultural district (M = 2.54, SD = 1.34), clear signs for traffic in culture district (M = 2.51, SD = 1.25), more arts shows and product rather than shops (M = 2.29, SD = 1.30), map of cultural district for guidance (M = 2.26, SD = 0.88), interactive cultural activities (M = 2.20, SD = 1.28), clear open time guidance for exhibition (M = 2.09, SD = 1.20), quality of food provided in cultural district (M = 2.06, SD = 1.00), quality of artists' skill in cultural district (M = 2.00, SD = 1.09) were perceived as the more important 10 attributes in 798 cultural district. As shown in Table 18, the most satisfied attribute were number of automatic selling machine (M = 3.20, SD = 0.90), the more satisfaction attributes are interactive culture activities (M = 2.60, SD = 1.06), clear signs for traffic in cultural district (M = 2.57, SD = 0.78), enough parking place in cultural district (M = 2.49, SD = 0.92), number of restaurants (M = 2.43, SD = 0.70), more art shows and product rather than shops (M = 2.43, SD = 0.88), clear open time guidance for exhibition (M = 2.34, SD = 0.94), map of cultural district guidance (M = 2.31, SD = 0.83), quality of food provided in cultural district (M = 2.29, SD = 0.83), quality of artists' skill in cultural district (M = 2.14, SD = 0.73) and number and quality of arts shows and activities (M = 2.11, SD = 0.68).

Chapter Three   Analysis of Cultural District in China

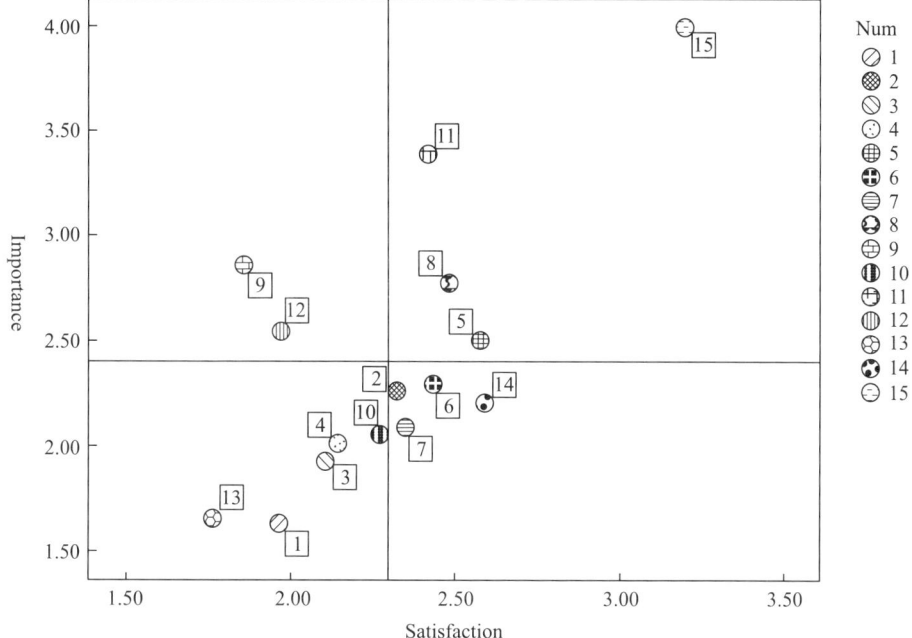

Notes:
1= Environment and cleanliness of the cultural district
2= Map of cultural district for guidance
3= Number and quality of arts shows and activities
4= Quality of artists' skill in cultural district
5= Clear signs for traffic in cultural district
6= More arts shows and product rather than shops
7= Clear open time guidance for exhibition
8=Enough parking place in culture district
9= Location of cultural district
10= Quality of food provided in cultural district
11= Number of restaurants
12= Layout of the cultural district
13= Uniqueness of culture district
14= Interactive cultural activities
15= Number of automatic selling machine

Diagram 7   The Scatter Pots for Results of Survey

2.3 Interpretation for the Results

Diagram 6 shows the result of data processing, each number of questions has been distributed in the different Quadrants, it could be explained base on current situation of 798 cultural district. Even some of results are unexpected, the study will try to recode them.

Firstly, 15 (number of automatic selling machine), 11 (number of restaurants), 8 (enough parking place in cultural district) and 5 (clear signs for traffic in cultural district) the four questions are in the Quadrant Two. Actually, all the four questions are the issues related to customers' service quality and facilities of 798 cultural district.

The reason why 15 in the maximum value of both importance and satisfaction is that the number of automatic selling machine in cultural district is limited and those respondents just use it, they think automatic selling machine is very convenient for buying goods at any time. This results seems tell us the number of automatic selling machine in cultural district is not enough potentially. On the other hand, 798 cultural district has attracted lots of tourists from all over the country, Particularly to the major holidays, the number of visitors is more higher than usual, 798 cultural district need to provide sufficient parking place and restaurant, as well as clear traffic sign, allows tourists to visit and walking in cultural district. While it is the tourists and 5, 15, 11, 8 cares very much for service projects, so that these issues in the first quadrant are more logical.

Secondly, 9 (Location of cultural district) and 12 (Layout of the cultural district) the two questions are in Quadrant One. It means that tourists are not satisfy with the two questions but they think the two question are more important, management level of 798 cultural district should keep concentrate on it. However, tourists are not satisfy with the location of cultural district probably they misunderstand the location of cultural district was appointed out by government rather than the outcome of artists getting together spontaneously. Layout of the cultural district is considered more important by tourists, because they more concern about those issues which can let them more easily look around 798 cultural district.

Thirdly, 1 (environment and cleanliness of the cultural district), 13 (uniqueness of cultural district), 3 (number and quality of arts shows and activities), 4 (quality of artists' skill in cultural district) and 10 (quality of food provided in cultural district) are in Quadrant Three. Environment and cleanliness of the cultural district is in the position of maximum neglect importance, it probably means that tourists mainly concentrate on what kind of activities cultural district can provide and whether they can enjoy this activities or not. Therefore, they don't concern about the importance of environment and cleanliness of the cultural district, but once they find anywhere's dirty they will be dissatisfy with it. Maybe the respondents didn't truly realize the specialty of 798 cultural district and they just give a hurried and cursory glance at cultural district. Just like mentioned, the main purpose of most of respondents come to 798 cultural district is for its reputation, they seldom care about quality of arts and artists' skill in cultural district, therefore, 3 and 4 are in the position of low importance and satisfaction. Generally speaking, most of tourists are not satisfy with the quality of food provided by scenic spot in China, they are not going to have lunch and dinner inside of cultural district at all, thus 10 is in the position of low importance and dissatisfaction.

Fourthly, 7 (clear signs for traffic in cultural district), 6 (more arts shows and product rather than shops) and 14 (interactive cultural activities) are in Quadrant Four. It is obvious that all the three issues are related to art works and activities in 798 cultural district, respondents basically don't care about it but these issues just mean a lot to art shops or galleries etc. therefore, they have higher satisfaction and lower importance.

3. Analysis for the Three Successful Cases

3.1 Stakeholder— A Frame of Theoretical Analysis

Stakeholder theory is suitable for analyzing and researching structure of participating or creating the same events related to the different interests of groups, and these groups will have different impact on the event that they participated and created. This theory has two levels, the first level focuses on the different roles of reference groups affect the whole event; the second level focuses on the different relationship of relevant interest groups in the project or event. According to Schemer, K (1999) "stakeholder analysis is a process of systematically gathering and analyzing qualitative information to determine whose interests should be taken into account when developing and/or implementing a policy or program". Schemer clearly describes the characteristics of the stakeholder, he stressed that this method fully collect and analyze information on the view of qualitative research, therefore, those attributes of reference group's interests and benefits should be considered during process of carrying out one project and policy.

Freeman stressed that this research and the approach mainly targets those groups or individuals who play important role for the success can affect specific group and individual. Different reference groups have different starting points and different influence power. In an event, different groups can be broken down into "basic reference group" and "peripheral reference group". Basic reference groups are used to tend to have a certain input in advance, there could be not events without their organizations and initiatives, a series of events or results often affect other reference groups, it is called peripheral groups. Reid S. & Arcodia C. (2002) said that direct or primary Stakeholders include employees, volunteers, sponsors, suppliers, spectators, attendees and participants in an event, people without whom the event would not exist. Secondary stakeholders include government, host community, emergency services, general business, media and tourism organizations who have an interest in an event programs, but who are not indispensable for event production. In the event of various stakeholder groups should have different levels and categories. These groups can be broadly classified into two categories, the basic reference groups should include employees, volunteers, sponsor, suppliers, audience attended and participants; peripheral groups includes the government, a site of project groups, emergency services, other services and etc.

In accordance with the theory of stakeholders and R&D, this study will clearly verify the different stakeholders and present to the Beijing 798 cultural district. The below table shows based relevant groups and peripheral related groups base on this theory. These groups will contain the 798 cultural district which is closely related to the interests of the various groups. It includes the provision of artistic creativity and talent with gallery and creative arts – related agent company groups, it also includes consumer and art products main tourists and audience. Peripheral stakeholder groups will be included at all levels of government and the relevant government departments related groups, this part of the groups also contains all of the related professional government departments such as the Ministry of Culture; the local population groups included in the local resident for at least 2 years of local residents. Commercial organizations groups mainly refers to the local hotels, restaurants, cafes, provide ancillary services business with the group also includes local banks, advertising, the media and other industries such as the 798 cultural and arts district commercial groups contributions.

Stakeholder theory stresses different stakeholder has different type of complaints, impact and expectations for one project and event. It is very crucial to study these different relevant groups, because it can clearly measure the effective development of policies, the persistence of relevant event's impact and some issues about the policies driving forces to other reference groups. These attributes greatly impact on the success of event. Event organizers must ensure that all stakeholder groups are gave a voice and therefore that they are all consulted. This enables stakeholder groups that are not as strong as some others to be heard (Sautter and Leisen, 1999). On the other side, stakeholder theory also suggests that the organizers of event or project must ensure all the

Chapter Three Analysis of Cultural District in China

reference group could be obtained and given equal speaking rights, it could be enquired suggestions equally. Thus, it ensures that a group sound will not too strong in a group. Freeman (1984) stress in further that "to be an effective strategist you must deal with those groups that can affect you, while to be responsive (and effective in the long run) you must deal with those groups that you can affect". It means that a successful strategy maker have to communicate with those groups which can influence him.

Table 16 798 Cultural and Arts District Related Group Divided and Contains the Description of the Component

Classification	Based relevant groups	Peripheral related group
Description	Art deductive talent group/Art Co Including: The arts talent group which includes art management talents, or call the arts company management personnel and other relevant staff	The Government and the various professional management groups Including: The provincial level, district and local government, the Government has also included the professional sectors, such as the ministry of culture and the financial support of the Government of the professional sector
	Tourists/audience cultural consumers groups Including: Domestic tourist and international tourists, for the first time to visit the 798 and the many tourists	Community residents and volunteers to groups Including: Local residents are included in the ordinary residents and volunteers, volunteer in society of the role and function of the increasingly obvious, especially since the beginning of a more widespread interest received
	Professional groups of non – profit organizations included: In accordance with the approval from the Government and register the various fund association and the organization of charitable fund such as the Association of non – profit organizations	Local profitable business organization groups Including: Local hotels, restaurants, etc. to provide services in support of the business groups, also includes a local advertisers, bank

3.2 Discussion for These Cases

The visitors of Avenue of the Arts Philadelphia in America basically include several different people because of the cultural facilities provided by the cultural district such as theaters, museums and art center etc. Firstly, the people who are interesting and love to get involve to art activities in local community, this cultural facilities attract them continue to consume so called cultural product. On the other hand, as the cultural district develops rapidly, lots of tourists come here for travelling; Certainly, Insa – Dong cultural district has really long history and government has invested very kinds of resources to make it become a cultural symbolization of local community. Particularly, it has successfully attracted thousands of tourists and visitors from all over the world in 1988 Olympic Game. Those customers who are interested in art works and antique collection also visit Insa – Dong cultural district; as to 798 cultural district, most people come to the district as a tourist because of its good reputation in recent years rather than seeking art works and exchanging. Secondly, creative class and the concept of creative talents appears in the mid of 1990s, this class is a new group, their main task is constant with new ideas and figure out better methods of doing things. The theory of creative class regards talents forces as a resource of creativity, these creative power drive the development of local economy and prosperity. As a result of this theory was generally recognized by Western countries and therefore artists group has been paid attention. In the last 10 years, there are general observation and recognition that some cities are able to attract and focus on many creative people who are attracted to come these places through the cultural facilities, cultural institutions, cultural activities and chance of employment such as London, Paris, New York, Los Angeles and other important cities in Western countries. However, it also includes some cities of China such as Beijing, Shanghai, Guangzhou etc. The results of cultural talent bringing together is the capability of attracting tourists. In particular, it is worth of stressing that the further attracting cultivate more and more outstanding creative talents come and enrich these cities' creative human capital. When running a cultural district, the interactive activities between artist and creative members of the cultural district will generate distinctions with other cultural districts, and it is the distinctions that can gain a competitive advantage. On the other hand, the history of the development of the Western countries, artists have played a major role in the shaping of urban life. Western countries city has undergone the process of life cycle some of them have redeveloped in nearly 20 years, artists and talent groups during this process has played an important role. The artists group in 798 cultural district has its own process of evolution.

　　Artists moved into 798 district originally and it not only changed the abandoned factory but also changed the fate of pulled down. Artist is 798 Art District pioneer, but it doesn't mean that they could be here all the time. Their presence in the region can allow a revitalization of the area in a short time and increase the rent appreciation. In turn, artists will also be forced to move to find next suitable place for survival because of the cost of living and noisy environment. These artists' getting together and dispersing can visually reflect the overall changing of artistic district. Artists' changing reflect the process of construction and deconstruction. It is also the process of keeping up seeking new balance between different business industrial and process of interest transformation. The following table can reflect the comparison of artistic talent groups of 798 cultural district moving in with other organization.

Table 17 The Changing of Artists and Talent Group Moving in (2010 – 2015)

Time	Artists workshops	Gallery	Other organizations (Design, Advertising, etc)	Food	Fashion shops	Total	Remarks
2010	21	9	13	3	4	50	
2011	43	15	19	6	6	89	
2012	46	21	34	8	9	118	
2013	57	88	47	17	19	228	
2014	49	133	52	26	20	280	
2015	29	154	46	35	70	334	

The table shows such a thing that the main reason the original development of 798 cultural district is some of artists established their own workshop base on five attributes:

(1) Low cost of renting house. According to the interview with artists, the artists group include those people who graduated in Beijing art school, break out of social system into freedom profession and come outside of Beijing for the reputation of this district. This sector of the population in Beijing is the main problem in finding cheap creative space. This from the information and to the artist's tracking interviews can be seen in the area of their choice, rents are generally relatively cheap and relatively remote location, convenient. It can be imagined that at that time a lot of street artists in life without guarantees that rent expenditure cheaper is better. At that time, 798 Art

District has not yet been established as the Cultural and Art District. In fact, it is a slice of abandoned factory and plant in a very poor condition, therefore, it has very cheap renting fees. Xu Yong, Wong Yui who early accessed to 798 cultural district and Chang xiaota and Fu lei have spoken of it. At that time, the dilapidation of the sense of 798 Zhang Xiao Hu Jintao also affected by this, they created a series of art works in the subject of city waste. According to Zhang xiaotao, this is the place of the coexistence of dream words and dumping ground. At that time, no one can image that they created the biggest gallery of China because of their getting together.

(2) These factories are spacious and very special. The spacious and bright plant and its unique structure are the other main reasons to attract early artist. Actually, it has been the artist began rental of space 798 cultural district before the formation of 798 art district. Initially, a failure to recognize the 798 Bauhaus architectural style building's value, aesthetic values and historical values, as well as its further development re-use value. Starting from 2005, other organizations such as the galleries gradually increased in 798 cultural district and the proportion of artists has declined. In terms of interview with those artists and talent group, the changes of 798 Art District are large and very fast, particularly this kind of changes will become very clear. Sometimes, there are several shops are opened in 798 Arts District in a short period of time. Of course, these new institutions mainly two categories: One is a coffee shop, others are commercial premises. Those organizations in 798 cultural district spoke of these phenomena, most people are expressing their concern and some people even expressed the unequivocal opposition. In the view of some people, 798 cultural district has become a tourism area for cheap commercial goods.

(3) Some scholars believe that cultural district seem to be distinct from other trades to become a separate field and have a significant impact on the economy of the independent areas (Lewis J., 1990). He pointed out that the production of cultural products became more effective, on the other hand, cultural district can maximize local social and economic impact. From the history of the development of the arts and cultural district, it is a more significant step to seek resources for promoting urban development and growth. Regeneration has become an important local planning standards and goals, and the status of that culture has been a growing tendency to economy, social and urban policies are linked closely. However, one important issue is by what way culture can revitalize an city's economy.

The "new economic theory" and "knowledge-based new economy" aroused extensive research (Bradford, N., 2002; Donal, B. and Morrow, 2003). This process emphasized on transformation of the pattern of "tradition" to "modern". Since the 1980s, the new company is driven by a knowledge-based industrial, particularly in the place of talent interchange and regional strip, thereby changing the model of resources determine geographical position. The expansion of the new economy has been orientated greatly as a creative economy or industrial center. In these new economic zones, knowledge, innovation and creativity are more production process than the result of production. Prosperity of new economic is reflect by cluster of geographic location.

Concept of economic – focused culture district was driven by the application of theory of "innovative level". Because of the common goal of economic development, this theory is related to research for cluster. The concept of Creative class and creative talents appears in the mid –1990s, this class means a new employee groups, their main task is to constantly seek out new ideas and better method. Theory of creative class positions the creative talent to be resources of creativity, these power of creativity drive prosperity of local economy. On the basis of these theories, cultural district can be refined to a few points as following:

The first, it is the urban construction which includes the rehabilitation of urban decay in the region to attract tourists, external investment and shape a positive image of the city. The second, it is to support cultural development. The third, it is necessary to strengthen the protection of artistic and cultural heritage. The fourth, it is the support of the city of creative and innovative development. The fifth, it is the formation and strengthening of the geographical indication or geographical image.

Those scholars who stress the importance of culture district should be the focus of economic maintained. Culture district should be a strong innovation and place of creative atmosphere, while it has a large number of competitive culture and creative industries, artists and arts organizations could get sustainable development on the view of economy. According to this view, innovation is a powerful driving force for strengthening development of local economy and they believed that these innovations could be quantified and measured. In addition, culture district with the other two functions are respectively from the requirements of new forms cooperation and the characteristics of local community. Reinforce various forms of cooperation, including public entertainers and art personnel, local development agencies, social services agencies or teaching, research and training institutions, urban planning and private investor and mutual cooperation, which are the purposes of socio – economic development, particularly it could be implemented through a series of cultural activities and other broader interaction between the activities. Local managers pay close attention to the continuing adaptation of cultural policy, thereby to meet the urban development objectives. In many parts of the world, national culture district is to encourage the cities and local governments as part of the resource groups.

(4) In the area of town planning, the degree of involvement of community culture and cultural life philosophy increasing has been becoming new measurement of art and cultural project. Cultural life is a important expression of community creativity activities in their everyday lives. It is also a expression of effective arts and culture capacity (Jackson, Cabois Sahel Rui, 2006). This view implicit various channels of public participation in cultural activities.

In fact, the planning process of community of popular participation in the local culture district is a key factor. That is the only way in which culture district could obtain potential cultural driving force and public support. During the construction of Western culture district, people have not been regarded as one component of cultural district initially. However, later it was found that certain people of community in a series of decision play important role. In order to fully express influence of art to community, one of key mission is to identify artist and traditional culture successor. These people organize art activities and encourage community people get involve to activities of community culture creativity. Artists in the process of creation, they have also given the opportunity to express their heartfelt wishes to communities. As most of the research clearly indicated (Jackson, 2003), such practice of the arts or themselves often is not recognized or not fully understood, and encourage in the practices of such activities are considered less than minimal, and only a very few typical project exception. Culture district or local community will be a part of society's overall, if we are going to achieve their own creative potential and take advantage of this creative for improving our communities. The arts and the concept of a culture need to be understood and cultural participation in the life of the community on the role of the better understanding while making it an example of change will become acute and urgent.

(5) What is the difference between Cultural and Arts business organizations and non‐profit from the cultural and arts organizations? In simple terms, the most common issue is business associations in some kind of art and culture to the specific content of production, the commercial interests of the purposes of the registration of a company and non‐profit organizations for the implementation of the community is for educational or

charitable purposes for registered organizations. In fact, no matter what their name and what the original intention of non-profit organizations have to arts and culture. They rely on their own operational earn 40 percent of their total income to 50 percent of commercial arts organizations which will give more consideration to their products quality and these products impacts on society. A commercial cultural product may be a book, a painting, one television program and a movie or a DVD. Provided that the cultural goods must produce profits, which means that the profits from tangible cultural goods or authorized in cultural rights and the total revenue must exceed the production, distribution and marketing of products they spend. While all of these are a non-profit organization problem to be concerned about, or non-profit cultural and arts organizations get to the concerns of the Government and of individuals to their financing.

At the same time we should also note that both of indirect contribution and its direct sales of art commercial companies were equal important to the economy. Indirect contribution included advertising, marketing, product design, image endorsement, management, construction, transport, food and beverage, etc. Many artistic input requires these indirect participation of consumption. For example, in order to attract new customers, even if the legitimacy of large companies concentrate on accounting and marketing strategies which they would require more information through preparation and design of non-recurrent attractive brochure. Although the two lead of the long-term trends are apparent, technology innovative footsteps accompanied by the media have become more flexible. Media in a visualization not printing of the direction of development and the company continues to merge, particularly in order to achieve maximum benefits in large and medium-sized enterprises on the beginning of arts and culture to the United.

Many diverse business organization accumulate funds and provide consumers with a variety of entertainment project that will be built city many of the most lively area. They have broadened the consumer groups and attracted the attention of the sponsors by providing secure popular cultural experience, including their investment points from suburban areas to attract urban culture district. Art and Entertainment culture district is often culture Industrial of important by-product of culture district the important local business organizations of the principal force seat. Table 17 show the comparison analysis for the cases as a summary following:

Table 18 The Comparison Analysis for the Three Cases

Cases	Tourists cultural consumer groups	Artists talent groups	The government and the various professional groups	The people in the community	Profitable business organization
Avenue of the Arts Philadelphia	People in local community and outside of Philadelphia	Philadelphia orchestra, academy of music	Avenue of the Arts Council	Participate and support the planning of revitalizing	Academy of Music Company, performing arts companies and some investment companies
Insa-Dong cultural district	Most Korean tourists regard Insa-Dong as a traditional culture district rather than connecting with historical background	The cultural district more like a fashion place than a art district by the Artists and gallery, they don't get involve into the management activities	Local government figure out a management plan, such as supporting planning, activities' development and establishment of residents union etc	The people in community of Insa-Dong seldom participate cultural districts activities and it doesn't have relative organization	Recent years profitable business organization increased such as shop, restaurants, etc
798 cultural district	Currently, most of tourists come to cultural district because of the reputation rather than collection and exchanging activities	Artists union organizes art exhibition and some exchange activities with outside of world	Seven star group and cultural district management committee is the main official organization	The people in community of 798 cultural district seldom participate activities and no relative organization	The number of profitable organizations have increased dramatically

Avenue of the art Philadelphia has different characteristics from both Insa-Dong and 798 cultural district. The people in this community also visit the art district and become cultural consumers, the artists and talents group in Avenue of the art Philadelphia exist as a form of organization, it doesn't like Insa-Dong and 798 cultural district's artists group who are basically exist by the form of individual, art association and art workshops. As to the government organization, Avenue of the art Philadelphia has a Art council and 798 cultural district established a management committee by Seven

Star group and government to manage cultural district. Insa – Dong has some organizations such as residential agreement. Planning and decision making comes from local government and Soul administration department; most of profitable business organizations in Avenue of the Art Philadelphia are something like performing art company, Academy of Music company and capital investment companies etc. 798 cultural district has similar profitable business company with Insa – Dong such as private galleries, shop and restaurants etc.

Chapter Four   Findings and Conclusion

The study from the United States, South Korea and China three arts and cultural district in the case description and analysis aimed at summing up and found that the success of the domestic operation of arts and culture to the core elements. End – use stakeholder importance – performance theory and analytical tools, for both dimensions, which is based on the theory of the stakeholders of the classification and the arts and cultural district successfully market operations elements and specific policies. In the meantime, through the Western cultural and arts district development literature review and comb or brush and found that lots of valuable conclusions of the arts and cultural district of operational practices have an important guiding significance.

1. Findings

The first, the study found that many factors can affect the success of culture district, the ability of the leadership is the most important among these factors. Sustainable development of culture district must include effective leadership, regardless of the leadership is belong to the public sector or enterprise, charities, non – profit organization or business of stock holders. They also must have a set of clear and priority development objectives; urban planners and regional managers must have a clear target and market positioning. Arthur Brooks & Rilander Kooler (2001) compared nine cities' cultural district and point out four factors which can affect the success of cultural district in further. It has four dimensions of controlling art activities and levels: ①how to manage cultural district; ②degree of public participation; ③the changing of cultural space; ④type of district arts and culture design.

Although people want to regard cultural division as unified whole, the fact is that they are all instability and changing. As we can see, cultural district has diversity, different organization, various purpose and scope. How to define the success of cultural district depends on definition of cultural district. In this context, the important question is whether it can describe the success of cultural district. The economic vitality of cultural institution is important indicators of success, it mainly respect to Frost – krumpf's description of first wave of culture district, including large – scale cultural mix area, important art organizations and arts entertainment district of the city. Management and operation of culture district is dominated by a series of sectors, including the Town Planning Board, cultural department and economic development sectors. All the research for success of cultural district proved that there are similar factors of success existed, and that is effective leadership and clear goals.

Another key issue is development path of cultural district. Generally speaking, the development path of cultural district has two ways, they are "top – down" or "bottom – up" approach, the former is generated by good planning, the latter is generated by freedom strategies and activities. Although it has difficulty of distinguishing the definition between the two types of cultural district, consumption as the subject of the culture district often depends on a huge investment of local government, and production of the main body of culture district is typically to historical and cultural or traditional culture as root causes. This pattern means that areas, communities, economic and cultural link closely, it is not able to completely break away from the local community in the abstract background with building elsewhere the same cultural enterprise organizations. The same conclusion also derived from the Organization for Economic Cooperation and Development 2005 Annual Report, which has emphasized and pointed out that the cultural district is not possible to exclude any of the traditional view of the backplane in a vacuum. Therefore, management of culture district also needs involvement of mutual stakeholder's power.

There are many things related to cultural district, it is impossible to use a simple command to manage all the things. These complicated factors include many elements such as balancing relevant stakeholders' relationships, status and role of various elements, balancing of public and private resources and relationship of internal organization. It is too hard to compare many factors, because sometimes we emphasize the Government and leadership of cultural district role of the more local organizations and institutions; but sometimes we also stresses the cultural industry park "Management Zone", which refers to the interactive decision – making process between various factors.

The second, we must also see in culture district in the area of the non – profit arts is not economic development initiatives, on the contrary, it frequently happened that the fiscal deficit and to rely on the government or individual financing in order to run. Although the art of urban regeneration in the plays a key role important even, a view that make people believe that the arts is the development of urban regeneration the key elements of the plan. However, it should be recognized that the non – profit arts cannot and should not be regarded as the revival of the city. We should be soberly aware of the fact that even the western countries like non – profit center for the Performing Arts Museum and the so – called culture district, its location in a number of municipalities is still is the marginalization of units of a non – economic development the main engine. As a provider of development financing for social and creative sectors of compelling value that they cannot be ignored, and the government will be building a large number of these talents and the local communities in the broad masses in urban regeneration plans in locations other than those. Arts and technology workers and arts and business does have promoted community economic development and the community's ability to transform. It is in this context that the Government should as interests of one of the Parties, make the appropriate supervision in order to stimulate the city life boasts the middle class families (as arts audiences backbone) cultural consumption market potential, and not in the practice of handling the weakening of creative infrastructure of value and capabilities. These same culture (Industrial) in the area of the other stakeholders that should be involved, which is also connected campus ultimate success or failure are the important factors.

At the same time through the study also found that in Western Cultures district area of the major source of contributions, with the globalization of art are closely related to the non – enterprise with the private sector accounted for a large proportion. And the non – profit organizations in which the role of the directly active in the arts and culture, funds, artist information services have played a great role in unexpected. From the 1980s, the national arts funding associations, the National People the financing of associations and other major private foundations are also beginning to re – evaluate their past method of funding for the arts, by changing the demographic information and art in mode. BrooK; Kushner (2001) concluded that the study of non – profit organizations for economic development, the cultural district genuinely has played an important role.

The third, a growing number of people in the community or the organization's spontaneous participation in cultural and arts activities at all levels such as the availability of funds at the support, policy support and prosperity. These activities are

Chapter Four   Findings and Conclusion

gradually becoming mainstream tendency shows that many western countries of cities and towns have culture district from an art organization – based mode to artists and small economies of the life. They also act as an important component of the strategy for recovery. Cultural atmosphere of culture district plays a vital role in the formation of a cultural atmosphere in the community. Recurring hold a grand opening of artistic and cultural activities, which is to make the art "live" in the community, so that the artistic performances and art forms, together with the ongoing refurbishment appropriate support and guidance, is a cultural atmosphere vital factor. Community people in the mainstream of popular culture are undoubtedly plays a vital role. From the outside, how will a campus, areas or cities the distinct features in the hearts of the people, thus creating the impression that the concept is recognized, or with regard to a party to the public feel or their "image" and "flag", that is, one of the parks, areas or cities in particular important cultural artistic atmosphere.

Culture Park, cluster with a variety of different areas of the inhabitants of the associated, including local and regional authorities for their active participation. Although the community level of arts and cultural participation is at the core of the life of the community, many policies makers, urban planners and arts implementer did not fully aware of the fact that the arts community should become the core and community building is an important component of essential importance. By cultural participation boot communities city on the investigation carried out by the evaluation and research clearly shows that the participation of the people in the arts and cultural activities for a variety of reasons, some in order to better integrate into the society, with the assistance of the Organization sponsored activities, in order to experience the artistic quality of in order to understand the history of another culture or period and still in order to celebrate the cultural heritage and religious belief, etc. In conclusion, as stated in the previous section, it was felt at the community cultural participation positive impact is the multi – stakeholder, such as the creation of social capital, the promotion of public participation, and the strengthening of community pride, enhanced local management and the promotion of economic development and to meet the other requirements of the community education.

In culture district, if strengthening cultural celebrity and art groups of potential synergy, in practice, ensure that the appropriate space in the vicinity of the artist, non – profit institutions as well as the small Arts Cultural Industries Company, or by changing the incentives or financial incentives, to encourage their creativity and so forth, would greatly benefit the development of the region. In addition, from a macroeconomic perspective, culture district should also increase the intensity of the possibility that the funds were not only to the development of facilities and also to flow to other projects, including support to the park's cultural projects, artists and other cooperation between the arts groups. In addition, as a number of non - profit organizations through project funding group and the surrounding artist to run out of space, or go to a certain area to nurturing local talent is the reason for some effective ways. In the wider cultural district or town planning process, the integration of the different stakeholders of the role, functions and role of the viewing angle to study clearly and not only the region as an economic catalyst with a process of reflection can improve Cultural district project development efficiency, while enabling local arts community more direct beneficiaries and growing.

The fourth, in the development of cultural district, the Government and the relevant government departments as one of the parties key stakeholders, to a certain extent is a decision - making role of the stakeholders and as the culture (Industrial Park) and the fostering of governance in their culture district in the course of development of the role in recent years of the trend toward the development of these new trends is manifested in the following aspects:

Urban Construction has gradually become aware of the need to adopt comprehensive measures. Especially in the area of cultural mix as the main characteristics of culture district and the government party that integrated approach is particularly necessary. In order to document your mixed area is the main features of the cultural industrial zone (in the various categories of stakeholders mutual contacts and become a problem as a whole, they in local government and the relevant government departments will, under the leadership of these groups and arts organizations to develop a culture district and the good development engine. For that reason, the government offers a wide range of comprehensive measures to help cultural district in the development of these measures, including the posting of the boot flags, guaranteeing security cost - effective service, parking appropriate public transport facilities.

The local government sector in relation to national or state or city government sectors, the cultural industrial zone (both from the policy in terms of financial support of all show a comparatively strong vigor and advantages of playing a larger made available). The planned culture district area is the community social structure, dynamic market is also a consequence of public policy, including planning, infrastructure and the results of the services. These culture district, the objectives of the zone in the government sector and its related policies that are more and burn the standard, including transport and infrastructure, allow audience can easily reach this culture district. There are a few research personnel (Hitters E. and Richards, 2002; Mommaas, 2004) view, the government department of public policy in the form of spontaneous culture (Industrial) in the establishment of the zone should be geared to the use of the infrastructure, which can be achieved by providing critical services of high quality, facilitate information flows and promoting the interrelated production of trust and cooperation between the local economy can ease the situation. For example Brown (2000) compared Sheffield culture district and Manchester music park area, pointed out that the latter's success is largely due to the introduction of a based on organic and bottom – up approach in the policy. So we can see that as the manager of the major art, policy makers and planners need to choose a healthy community, the Out of as well as the necessary, more fully in the way that it handles to the community as well as the campus in the arts and cultural works to adopt a new way of working. There are some cities on the Government side and the use of Culture district a bit different from the nature of these issues, such as the question of unused space which mainly refers to the city center and the main street. As a result of a large commercial center and overall entertainment infrastructure development in these old centers and the main street of lost its status as a shopping and transport. In the city center area of the main features of the cultural industrial complex, district planning precisely in order to recovery from the vibrant City Center and Avenue to retake the shopper and consumer.

The fifth, the artists of the original acceptable is a traditional funding model, namely private charitable and public charity mixed together, are funded by artists and non – profit arts organizations commissioned to do the architectural, painting, performances, as well as co – art and design, such as the sculptures, monuments or boot flags such construction. These projects, artistic works and performances found buyers and viewers, and also in the operation of the artist as the subject of the large and small non – profit arts and cultural organizations provided support. Under such circumstances, many artists around the building of culture district may not necessarily be the adjacent, but as the artist work and living areas characterized by. In these regions, artists first moved into these has gone downhill in areas within the rent very low and spacious and brightly lit conditions conducive to the creation of Modern Art. However, these first moved into these places and a new look of artists had finally to prices and property tax increases, moving away from these places to have become increasingly popular. The best known of the Manhattan layer under when SoHu area during the twentieth century in the 1970s, a number of artists have jointly established a grass‐roots community culture district, through illegal means to enter this empty space with good lighting conditions and lower prices. Through their continuous efforts, SoHu without as the district trend artists concentrate, and is a very interesting residential area. In the end, in the creation of a climate of so popular, they were rising housing prices. Therefore, although SoHu area in people's minds and a state of the Art Zone, in fact, in this large retail area has been almost no artists.

Artists in various government acceptable assistance and no longer simply be the art of aesthetics, education and social value of investment on the part of the donor community, but favors art economic benefits brought by the donor. The art research on the impact of economic development with a view to confirming the legitimacy of public investment in these discussions is normally divided into layers, these include the public funding and other income includes the sale of tickets, works of art and artistic for trading, restaurant income, Hotel letting and so on. The R&D and even other clearly also relate to the state of the art in investment and lower crime rate, which in turn contacts to examine how the enterprises to boot to a particular region. The establishment of the cultural district and economic development of the affected have important synchronization, the focus that the artists from non‐profit organizations of the funding mode to the economic development as the center of the pattern. Although many people accused of the economic impact of the study on the excessive exaggerated public and private art in the return on investment, such a study itself really helped many summary makers center built for art look at the mode.

2. Conclusions

Although there are a large number of factors exist related to cultural district, culture district has only two of the "top‐down", one of which is the "bottom‐up". In this connection, from the perspective of cooperation most scholars who remain divided, people believe that "top down". This mode is not likely to succeed; another part that can be successfully, but there must be the underlying forces involved, the

Chapter Four　　Findings and Conclusion

implementation of participatory management of culture district development the only viable path. From a geographical perspective, there are also extremely rich possibilities that culture district of the geographical scope of the large cities of the entire small a community, or from the urban area to several cities in with the "Area" (in many international and regional concept can across the city and town, even across provincial and municipal). Moreover, culture district is available from industrial waste plant in the erection, also from the new construction of planning, of course, not be prohibited in the specified good regional and building development.

In a strict sense, culture district includes only the artistic and cultural activities, but sometimes it is also included in the part of the leisure and entertainment, and there are also various forms of culture and the arts, cultural activities from production and cultural activities of the pure consumption to cultural services; from stage to visual arts to the music to the media; from the cafes and restaurants to health and fitness center. Cultural enterprises typically are not very large size, this is determined by the nature of the cultural activities, with the exception of a very few exceptions, most cultural enterprises are small or medium in size. The fact confirmed that culture district is not only a vertical relationship exists, and the move of the existence of a large number of colonies of horizontal relations, because the total is the source of creativity, so unique cultural resources of the essence of the Council for other products that add value chains of production. Many of the key features of the compulsory one element in the company, for example, research centers, training centers and cultural research and clear institutions, public development agencies or local management institutions and so on, so that the culture district can get the external economic environment, and it can make within the campus of various factors take full advantage of the external economic environment, the network of relationships, or directly with only the strengthening of cultural resources or related to the development of many of the cultural activities of a possible.

The culture district management there seems to be a number of issues of concern, these issues include the following: Public and private factors; the interrelationship between their respective between the status and role of the institutions of governance; innovation; campus network between the internal corporate relations framework; and the different cultural activities between the mutual cooperation and mutual coordination, and so on. These problems so that sometimes we had to use the word "Government" in place of "acting", and of course the Government refers to a series of all levels of management, as well as a series and urban and regional planning phase is the "Tools", and culture district management, the real significance should be based on a series of contracts, conventions and social network project practices. The different parts of the world culture district the experience of the development of the district and case analysis, the results display, it seems to be very difficult to identify a culture district development at the heart of the success of the special elements of success, because cultural and arts district has emerged in the development of its own too many diversified. Although such diversification has its own advantages, but for its research and clear objectives were far from conclusive. We are dealing here with research shows regional development there are too many different elements, each of them has the different perspectives to affect culture district development path.

3. Policies and Recommendations

3.1 Policies

Taking a general look at all the examples of western countries in the prevailing culture (Industrial) zone or a related regional building in which the Government and the relevant departments of the involvement is indispensable. Although the Government of many parts of the world has already started to investment – related funding sources for the maintenance of cultural district, government and stakeholders and decision – makers how to support a culture district development is still questionable. Through the study found that public policy should attach importance to and nurturing of existing cultural background of the arts and culture in the bud, i. e. All constitute a geographical region characteristics of these cultural and social factors, they are invariably moment is a special kind of things, constituting a culture district development potential base. Therefore, local governments should take appropriate action to adopt in order to investigate and understand the overall economic order, awareness and understanding of the "embryonic" (Powell and Alan, Gothic, 2004), this process and procedures is essential, because it can enable policy makers to better align their intervention and find the spontaneous development of the cultural background and the necessary degree of government intervention in the fine – tuning between balance. In Turin, Italy, in the case of the importance which they attached to the bottom – up approach, this method can be a government to the identity of the supplier of the emergence of investment to the "soft infrastructure", such as for the region of the perpetrator of the mutual exchange of unofficial network platform, picking up to focus on cultural district and local traditions, values and history of the close relationship between the Strategy.

This research recommends that governments at all levels should proceed from the local construction of "monument" landmark building into a local culture activities as the core of the boot. In the cultural district during the construction of the public investment in the income for not spectacular, impressive large engineering or construction, but through the establishment of community – based platform to help campus participation of all stakeholders in the development of a collaborative relationship with autonomy. Culture district of the activities of the natural result of all stakeholders the mutual understanding and promote a number of actors in cooperation and exchanges, thus enabling those previously may not know each others presence between related parties have the necessary exchange and cooperation, while at these districts in the arts and cultural activities are also being conceived and revealed the campus of operators and local officials, policy makers and relationship of managers. Western countries cultural district project in the functioning and development of good primarily due to the following reasons:

The first is to government departments such as the stakeholders and policy makers recognize that recognized culture (Industrial Park) located in the field presence of the vitality of the arts and cultural activities. Local decision makers must take appropriate action to recognize and to dig even local cultural scene. This kind of "embryonic", this goal through close observation and monitoring all active local scene activities is where you can find and achieved.

The second is the government stakeholders, public policy and local characteristics between the dependencies. Countless case table that public policy should focus on development, use of previously already exists in the bud, that is to say, all of these cultural and social factors that have a unique regional characteristics, constitutes a culture district development potential. In other words, when public policy was not used in one from scratch with the development of Cultural Park on the project, but used in the development of human rights by the local art scene, public policy in this state can bring their effectiveness. This does not mean that there needs to be a well – developed art scene, but a more cultural district needed for development, and fertile ground, the dynamics of soil of these congenital condition to rely solely on the adoption of the public bodies intervention that will not germinate take root. In addition cultural cluster and local linkages between the environments should also take full account of the factors. In fact, the only truth, and unique nature of cultural industries to be able to attract viewers of the main reasons, only found with these basic conditions of "very", will be able to be local communities and external potential audience as authentic. Thus, according to the results of the study to find this sample has the potential, to consolidate and develop a strong with local geographical, social and cultural background of the globalization of industrial park, public policies can be more effective.

The third, it is necessary to pay attention to the cultural industries of the academic community in the accumulation and the new economic research on the effects of the results into. The scholars have comprehensive measure of the proposed development of all of the project's potential costs and benefits of their final conclusion is that the development of large - scale projects just from the economic point of view is not justified. But it is a fact that the cultural industry's economic returns with a defective, accurate measurement and exaggerated by the conclusion of the study, the Government and the community to Other Stakeholders Investing and supported the city or in the campus large cultural facilities in the construction of these facilities are built after requires a lot of routine maintenance and operation of subsidies, they have not only to bring the commitments of the urban economic incentives, rather than in the real world manifestations of is that they often constantly demand operating subsidy, but they do not provide proof of the existence of these subsidies and sufficient reason.

The fourth is the Government try to increase the effectiveness of intervention on the part of public authorities, it must pay attention to the critical inputs or "soft base infrastructure" such as the full range of services, education and training facilities, funding and so on, it is of the utmost importance that you want to boot the promotion of local culture and the arts. To indicate the formation of the network structure, help the exchange of information and the promotion of confidence - building and the promotion of cooperation. If cultural policy is applied in this project, it may greatly enhance its effectiveness.

3.2 Recommendations

In general, the adoption of the above - mentioned case analysis and the stakeholders of the comprehensive studies and research, the study of the Government in the successful

Chapter Four Findings and Conclusion

operation of arts and cultural district in the recommendations are as follows:

The first, the promotion of our " as the product of the arts and of citizens as a guardian paradigm " act as part of the participants in the process and citizens of the arts of the transfer. The public should be linked to the self – education and self – improvement of the ideological and artistic and the connection which will enable us to make the arts and cultural prosperity and sustainable development.

The second, the government should focus on community gathering place, rather than simply the building of cultural facilities. The Government should endeavor to improve the community cultural infrastructure to enable these cultural facilities to truly become important gathering place for where people meet, interactive, and provide an opportunity to understand each other through a variety of ways to encourage the public to actively participate in cultural and artistic activities, thus developing a significant proportion of the pluralist community. In such places in which citizens can participate in cultural and arts, as well as the relevant social network, from which you make new friends; and the arts and cultural community can use a variety of wonderful way organizations, development and rendering and reproduction, thereby achieving their communities live in the "Today"; at the same time the citizens must constantly remind myself of civic awareness, so that they combine the historic and rich cultural heritage and continue to challenge yourself and creative, innovative expression, above and beyond their current status, entered a new cultural artistic expression.

The third, in addition to using a variety of methods to encourage the public to participate actively in arts and culture, the Government should in the city's cultural (Industrial Park) district planning for the construction of the public was broader and deeper democratic participation of civil society in general may provide adequate.

The fourth, the formulation of appropriate measures to ensure that the arts and cultural bodies in the establishment of the rich cultural activities, guide them to focus their efforts on the social contribution and how are they going to more vigor, and not just why do they need the financial community to support their plans.

The fifth, development of culture (Industrial Park) district organizations capacity. This is a cultural (Industrial Park) of the building is an important component, including, in particular, the establishment of effective volunteer recruitment and training programs.

The sixth, local leaders should pay attention to the shift of the economic – development priorities, namely from "economy" to extract a more constructive and sustainable economy, the expression rather than focusing on the development of the creative economy. Cultural Tourism and economic development, it is necessary to strike a balance. Sometimes it is not cultural tourism economy is the best, to begin slowly to help the public cultivate their cultural tourism – related economic and legal sense, facts have proved that, once they recognize that these travel concept works, they will ensure that its sustainable development.

The seventh, In order to make an effective marketing planning, the first step is to divide customers into different types. Base on the survey in this study, the customers could be classified two groups, one group is tourist who come to cultural district just for looking around because of the cultural district's reputation; other group is those people who are interesting in culture & art works and getting involve to art activities. It is obvious that the cultural district must develop marketing planning for different groups respectively. As to the first group, the marketing planning should more focus on those attributes related to service quality such as number of restaurants, quality of food provided in cultural district, clear open time guidance for exhibition, enough parking place in culture district and map of cultural district for guidance etc. It is very important to improve these attributes to meet the needs of customers, and these factors should be considered carefully by managers. The marketing planning will be made for the second customer group totally different, because they more focus on art works and cultural activities when they come to cultural district. These marketing planning include providing more exhibition shows, interactive with artists, art educating programs, through the various activities to attract people to get involve the cultural district. The cultural district should also advertise in public to strength cultural district's reputation in the world.

The eighth, in essential, cultural district has become an economic equity for local development. How can planners and manager intervene to maximize the benefits of revitalization generated by cultural district? How can policy address the types of market failure associated with culture – based revitalization? Thus, planners should begin with the commitment to "do no harm". We must remember that cultural district are largely self – organized. Ultimately, their success will stem from the commitment of those involved in creating them, not from some outside entity. Still, there are ways of supporting these grassroots initiatives (Stern and Seifert, 2007a, 2008).

(1) There is a clear rationale for social investment. Given the significant positive externalities associated with cultural district, investment strategies that are profit –

Chapter Four Findings and Conclusion

seeking, not necessarily profit – maximizing, could pay huge dividends to both the investors and the general community. Small loans for predevelopment and bridge financing, especially if linked to technical assistance, could increase the success rate of individual enterprises and clusters in general.

(2) The public sector can contribute to the viability fcultural district simply by doing its job better. Providing security, clean and safe streets, usable public spaces, convenient transit, and consistent and honest enforcement of zoning and development regulations would make the world much easier for those trying to seed and cultivate cultural district. Strategic grants for place – making activities—such as distinctive streetscapes and lighting, community and park facilities, and local fairs or festivals—would also provide returns greater than their costs.

(3) Urban economic policy makers should explore workforce development strategies that provide young people interested in the creative and cultural industries with the information and resources to make good decision about entering the fields. Whether that means integrating business courses into the curricula of creative arts high schools or developing apprenticeship programs for craft and technical occupations, improving the fit between creative sector opportunities and the interests of young residents of low – wealth communities is critical to improving the labor market and reducing the economic inequality currently associated with the arts. Although work – force development policies are not place – specific, neighbor – hood cultural district could serve as sites for artists' centers (Markusen and Johnson, 2006) or technical training programs as well as provide an excellent point of entry for connecting with young adults as they make decisions about their future.

(4) They need planners and researchers to help refine our statistical tools for monitoring the life history of cultural district. Up grading the measurement of the index components for cultural district's performance would clearly improve its accuracy and utility. Developing tools to track the level of economic transactions and the breadth and intensity of artistic social networks would greatly enhance the performance. Ideally, construction of a longitudinal database with both individual and neighborhood indicators would enable assessment of the benefits and costs of culture – based revitalization to people as well as places. As a complement, qualitative research and comparative case study of cultural district would advance our understanding of their dynamics and under what conditions they emerge, decline or thrive. Cultivating cultural district can be but one approach to community planning and regional economic development policy.

However, given their potential for generating social benefits beyond purely commercial success as well as their strategic importance to the health of a city and region's creative economy, nurturing neighborhood cultural district is a strategy that deserves the attention of government, philanthropy and the private sector.

Appendix A

How important are these features?

Extremely important	Very important	Important	Slightly important	Not important
1	2	3	4	5

Number	Attributes Description	1 2 3 4 5
1	Environment and cleanliness of the culture district	
2	Map of culture district for guidance	
3	Number and quality of arts shows and activities	
4	Quality of artists' skill in cultural district	
5	Clear signs for traffic in culture district	
6	More arts shows and product rather than shops	
7	Clear open time guidance for exhibition	
8	Enough parking place in culture district	
9	Location of cultural district	
10	Quality of food provided in culture district	
11	Number of restaurants	
12	Layout of the culture district	
13	Uniqueness of culture district	
14	Interactive culture activities	
15	Number of automatic selling machine	

How well did the culture district perform?

Very dissatisfy	dissatisfy	Fair	Satisfy	Very satisfy
1	2	3	4	5

Number	Attributes Description	1 2 3 4 5
1	Environment and cleanliness of the culture district	
2	Map of culture district for guidance	

continued table

Very dissatisfy	dissatisfy	Fair	Satisfy	Very satisfy
1	2	3	4	5

Number	Attributes Description	1 2 3 4 5
3	Number and quality of arts shows and activities	
4	Quality of artists' skill in cultural district	
5	Clear signs for traffic in culture district	
6	More arts shows and product rather than shops	
7	Clear open time guidance for exhibition	
8	Enough parking place in culture district	
9	Location of culture district	
10	Quality of food provided in culture district	
11	Number of restaurants	
12	Layout of the culture district	
13	Uniqueness of culture district	
14	Interactive culture activities	
15	Number of automatic selling machine	

Appendix B

Interview Record in 798 Cultural District (Artist)

Interviewee	Sex	Province	Occupation	Time	Place	Duration (min)	Remark
Unknown	Male	Sichuan	Artist	2015.7	798 cultural district		
Fang Min	Male		Artist	2015.7	Shang zun workshop	20	
Gao Xian	Male	Shandong	Artist	2015.7	Artist workshop	95	
Hao Guang	Male		Artist	2015.7	798 cultural district	43	
Huang Rui	Male		Artist	2015.7	Artist workshop	61	Planer of 1-3 Art Festival 798 cultural district
Mr. Ba	Male		Artist	2015.7	Mr. Ba workshop	6	
Li Jiushi	Male	Shandong	Artist (oil panting)	2015.7	Artist workshop	84	
Li Zhengwei	Male		Artist (oil panting)	2015.7	Red Art workshop	23	798 cultural district
Sheng Haoyu	Male		Artist (Design)	2015.7	Shang gong space	58	
Shi Guorui	Male	Shanxi	Artist (Design)	2015.7	North five highway workshop	15	
Sun Furong	Female		Artist	2015.7	Zhang xiaotao workshop	20	Song zhuang artist

Interview Record in 798 Cultural District (Galleries & Other organizations)

Organization	interviewee	Sex	Age	Time	Place	Duration (min)	Remark
	Director Liang	Male	41	2015.7	Democratic Alliance Beijing	25	

continued table

Organiza-tion	interv-iewee	Sex	Age	Time	Place	Duration (min)	Remark
	Li Zheng	Male	36	2015.7	Administration Office 798 cultural district	65	Director of 798 cultural district committee
3 plus 3 art space	Miss. Guo	Female	28	2015.7	3 plus 3 art space office	26	
BRDR		Male		2015.7	798 cultural district		
Some shops		Male		2015.7	Shops	40	

References

[1] Aas, C., Ladkin, A., & Fletcher, J. Stakeholder Collaboration and Heritagemanagement. Annals of Tourism Research, 2005, 32 (1): 28 –48.

[2] Adams, C., Bartelt, D., Elesh, D., Goldstein, I., Kleniewski, N., & Yancy, W. Philadelphia: Neighborhoods, Divisions and Conflict in a Postindustrial city. Philadelphia: Temple University Press, 1991.

[3] Adde, L. Nine Cities: The Anatomy of Downtown Renewal. Washington, D. C. : Urban Land Institute, 1969.

[4] Agranoff, R., & McGuire, M. American Federalism and the Search for Models of Management. Public Administration Review, 2001, 61 (6): 671 –681.

[5] Agranoff, R., & McGuire, M. Collaborative Public Government: New Strategies for Local Government. Washington, D. C. : Georgetown University Press, 2003.

[6] Ann Markusen and Anne Gadwa. Arts and Culture in Urban or Regional Planning: A Review and Research Agenda. Journal of Planning Education and Research, 2009, 29 (3): 379 –391.

[7] Anna Maria Bounds Network Management in Cultural District Implementation: The Case of Philadelphia's Avenue of the Arts. Degree of Doctor of Philosophy, 2006.

[8] Antoine le blanc. Cultural Districts, a New Strategy forRegional Development? The South –East Cultural District in Sicily. Regional Studies, 2010, 44 (7): 905 –917.

[9] Arnaboldi, M., & Spiller, N. Actor Network Theory and Stakeholder Collaboration: The Case of Cultural Districts. Tourism Management, 2011, 32 (3): 641 –654.

[10] Associated Councils for the Arts. Americans and the Arts: A Survey of Public Opinion. New York: Author, 1975.

[11] Baltzell, E. D. Philadelphia Gentleman. New Brunswick, NJ: Transaction, 1958.

[12] Baltzell, E. D. Puritan Boston and Quaker Philadelphia. New York: Free Press, 1979.

[13] Bassett, K. Urban Cultural Strategies and Urban Regeneration: A Case Study and Critique. Environment and Planning A, 1993 (25): 1773 – 1788.

[14] Bassett, K. R. Griffiths and I. Smith. Cultural Industry, Cultural Clusters and the City: The Example of Natural History Film – making in Bristol, Geoforum, 2002 (33): 165 – 177.

[15] Bauman, J. Wilson Goode: The Black Mayor as Urban Entrepreneur. Journal of Negro History, 1992, 77 (3): 41 – 158.

[16] Beauregard, Robert A. City Planning and Postwar Regime in Philadelphia. In M. Lauria(Eds.). Reconstructing Urban Regime Theory. Thousand Oaks, CA: Sage, 1997.

[17] Beauregard, Robert A. City profile: Philadelphia Cities, 1989, 6 (4): 300 – 308.

[18] Bennett, William J. The Index of Leading Culture Indicators Carmichael, CA: Touchstone Books, 1994.

[19] Berelowitz, J. Protecting High Culture in Los Angeles: MOCA and the Ideology of Urban Redevelopment. The Oxford Art Journal, 1993, 16 (1): 149 – 157.

[20] Berreman, G. D. Anemic and Emetic Analysis in Social Anthropology. American Anthropologist, 1966 (68): 346 – 354.

[21] Besculides, A. , Lee, M. E. , & McCormick, P. J. Residents' Perceptions of Thecultural Benefits of Tourism. Annals of Tourism Research, 2002, 29 (2): 303 – 319.

[22] Bissinger, B. A Prayer for the City. New York: Random House, 1997.

[23] Bounds, A. Lessons Learned from Riverhead, New York's Arts District. Paper Presented at the Urban Affairs Association Annual Meeting. Detroit, 2000.

[24] Bradford, N. Creative Cities Structured Policy Dialogue Backgrounder Canadian, Canadian Policy Research Networks, Ottawa, 2004.

[25] Bramwell, B. , & Sharman, A. Collaboration in Local Tourism Policymaking. Annals of Tourism Research, 1999 (26): 392 – 415.

[26] Breiter D. and Milman A. Attendees' Needs Andservice Priorities in a Large Convention Center: Application of the Importance – performance Theory. Tourism Management, 2006, 27 (6): 1364 – 1370.

[27] Bronner, E. B. Village into Town, 1701 – 1746. In R. F. Weigley, N. B.

References

Wainwright, & E. Wolf 2nd (Eds). Philadelphia: A 300 – Year History. New York: W. W. Norton & Company, 1982: 33 – 67.

[28] Brookings Institute. Philadelphia in Focus: A Profile from Census. Washington, DC: Author, 2003.

[29] Brooks, A. C. and R. J. Kushner. Culture Districts and Urban Development, International Journal of Arts Management, 2001, 3 (2): 4 – 15.

[30] Brown, A., O'Connor, J., Cohen, S. Local Music Policies within a Global Music Industry: Cultural Quarters in Manchester and Sheffield. Geoffrey, 2000 (31): 437 – 451.

[31] Canadian Heritage. Department of Canadian Heritage—home, Available online at www. pch. gc. ca/index_ e. cfiii, accessed 24 July, 2007.

[32] Carl Grodach. Beyond Bilbao: Rethinking Flagship Cultural Development and Planning in Three California Cities. Journal of Planning Education and Research, 2010, 29 (3): 353 – 366.

[33] Carlson, L. Policy Networks as Collective Action. Policy Studies Journal, 199, 28 (3): 502 – 520.

[34] Carta, M. Structure Territorial of Strategic Cultural Support, Economic of Culture, 2004, 14 (1): 39 – 56.

[35] Caves. Richard E. Creative Industries: Contracts between Arts and Commerce. Cambridge: Harvard University Press, 2000.

[36] Center for Arts and Culture. America's Cultural Capital: Recommendations for Structuring the Federal Role. Washington, DC: Center for Arts and Culture, 2001.

[37] Cheng, S. – W. Cultural Goods Creation, Cultural Capital Formation, Provision of Cultural Services Andcultural Atmosphere Accumulation. Journal of Cultural Economics, 2006: 263 – 286.

[38] Cheng – Yi Lin and Woan – Chiau Hsing. Culture – led Urban Regeneration and Community Mobilization: The Case of the Taipei Bao – an Temple Area, Taiwan, 2008.

[39] Cherbo, Joni M. A Department of Culture Resources: A Perspective on the Arts, Journal of Arts Management, Law and Society 22, 1992 (1): 44 – 63.

[40] China. Eisenhardt, K. Building Theories from Case Study Research. Academy of Management Review, 1989 (14): 532 – 550.

[41] Chua, W. F. Experts, Networks and Inscriptions in the Fabrication of Accounting Images: A Story of the Representation of Three Public Hospitals. Accounting,

Organizations and Society, 1995, 20 (2/3): 111 - 145.

[42] City of Vancouver. Live/Work and Work/Live: Vancouver Overview, Available Online at http: //vancouver. ca/ctyclerk/cclerk/960416/sp3 - htm, accessed 24 July, 2007.

[43] Clark, J. S., Jr., & Clark, D. J. Rally and Relapse, 1946 - 1968. In R. E. Weigley, N. B. Wainwright, & E. Wolf 2nd (Eds) . Philadelphia: A 300 - Year History. New York: W. W. Norton & Company, 1982.

[44] Culture as an Engine of Local Development Process: System - Wide Cultural Districts: Prototype Cases. Growth and Change, 2012, 44 (4): 571 - 588.

[45] Daein Art Market Project Nuetinamusup. Pocket Information. Gwangju: Daein Art Market Project [in Korean], 2011.

[46] Daughen, J. R., & Binzen, P. The Cop Who would be King: The Honorale Frank Rizzo. Boston: Little, Brown and Company, 1977.

[47] Davide Ponzini, Silvia Gugu, Alessandra Oppio (2014). Is the Concept of the Cultural District Appropriate for Bothanalysis and Policymaking? Two Cases in Northern Italy. City, Culture and Society 5, 2014: 75 - 85.

[48] Deng, W. Using a Revised Importance Performance Analysis Approach: The Case of Taiwanese Hot Springs Tourism. Tourism Management, 2007, 28 (5): 1274 - 1284.

[49] Denzin, N., & Linconln, Y. Entering the Field of Qualitative Research. In N. Denzin & Y. Lincoln (Eds.) . Handbook for Qualitative Research. Thousand Oaks, CA: Sage, 1994.

[50] Dimaggio, Paul. Managers of the Arts. Washington, DC: NEA Research Report no. 20, 1987.

[51] Dimaggio, P. & Useem, M. The Arts in Class Reputation. In M. W. Apple (Eds.) . Cultural and Economic Reproduction in Education: Essays on Class, Ideology and the State. London, Boston and Henley: Routledge and Kegan Paul, 1982.

[52] Dimaggio, P. Social Structure, Institutions and Cultural Goods: The Case of the United States. In P. Boudieu & J. S. Coleman (Eds) . Social Theory for a Changing Society. Boulder, CO: Westview Press, 1991.

[53] Dimaggio. The Vital Border of Culture Policy Studies. In the Arts in a New Millennium: Research and the Arts Sector (Eds.) . Valerie B. Morris and David B. Pankratz. Westport, CT: Praeger, 2003.

[54] Donal, B. and D. Morrow. Competing for Talent: Implications for Social

and Cultural Policy in Canadian City – regions, a Report Prepared for Strategic Research and Analysis, Strategic Planning and Policy Coordination, Department of Canadian Heritage, 14 May, 2003.

[55] Douglas S. Noonan. How US Cultural Districts Reshape Neighbourhoods. Cultural Trends, 2013, 22 (3–4): 203–212.

[56] Dreezen, C. Community Cultural Planning; A Guidebook for Community Leaders. Washingto, DC: Americans for the Arts, 1998.

[57] Dubini, P. and Raviola, E. Geography of Media Industries: Trends and paradoxes. Some Evidence from Italy. Paper Presented at the 7th World Media Economics Conference. Beijing, 2006.

[58] Edwards, B., Goodwin, M., Pemberton, S., & Woods, M. Partnership Working in Rural Regeneration: Governance and Empowerment. Bristol: Policy Press in Association with the Joseph Rowntree Foundation. European Planning Studies, 2000, 19 (8).

[59] Eleonora Lorenzini. The Extra – urban Cultural District: An Emerging Local Production System: Three Italian Case Studies, 2010.

[60] Ellis, P. H. The Politics of Bread and Circuses: Building the City for the Visitor Class. Urban Affairs Review, 2000, 35 (3): 316–333.

[61] Erickson. Cultural Planning: An Urban Renaissance? London: Routledge, 1986.

[62] Evans, G., and J. Foord. Cultural Mapping and Sustainable Communities: Planning for the Arts Revisited. Cultural Trends, 2008, 17 (2): 65–96.

[63] Evans, G. Cultural Planning. An Urban Renaissance? London: Routledge, 2001.

[64] Evans, G. Measure for Measure: Evaluating the Evidence of Culture's Contribution to Regeneration. Urban Studies, 2005, 42 (5–6): 959–983.

[65] Farrell, B., & Twining – Ward, L. Reconceptualizing Tourism. Annals of Tourism Research, 2004 (2): 274–295.

[66] Florida, Richard. Cities and the Creative Class. New York: Routledge, 2005.

[67] Florida, Richard. The Rise of the Creative Class. New York: Basic Books, 2002.

[68] Flyvbjerg. Making Social Science Matter. Cambridge: Cambridge University Press, 2001.

[69] Frederic Le Play. Cultural Quarters as Mechanisms for Urban Regeneration. Part I: Conceptualising Cultural Quarters. Planning, Practice & Research, 1882, 18 (4): 293 – 306.

[70] Freeman, R. E. Strategic Management: A Stakeholder Approach. Boston: Pitman, 1994.

[71] Frost – Krumpf, Hilary Anne. Cultural Districts: the Arts as a Strategy for Revitalizing Our Cities. Washington, DC: Americans for the Arts, 1998.

[72] Furnweger, K. Shedd Aquarium: Then and Now. Chicago: Shedd Aquarium Press, 1999.

[73] Galligan, Ann M., and Joni Maya Cherbo. Financial Support for Individual Artists: Report to the National Endowment for the Arts, October, 2003.

[74] Gans, H. Popular Culture and High Culture: An Analysis and Evaluation of Taste. New York: Basic Books, 1974.

[75] Garcia, B. Cultural Policy and Urban Regeneration in Western European Cities: Lessons from Experience, Prospects for the Future. Local Economy, 2004 (19): 312 – 326.

[76] Gaskell, G. Individual and Group Interviewing. In M. W. Bauer & G. Gaskell (Eds.). Qualitative Researching with Text, Image, and Sound, 2000: 38 – 56.

[77] Gendron, Y., Cooper, D. J., & Townley, B. The Construction of Auditing Expertise in Measuring Government Performance. Accounting, Organizations and Society, 2007 (32): 101 – 129.

[78] Ghafele, R., & Santagata, W. Cultural Tourism and Collective Trademarks: The Case of Byblos and Saida, Lebanon. Working Paper. International Centre for Research on the Economics of Culture, Institutions and Creativity, 2006.

[79] Giddings, F. H. The Scientific Study of Human Society in the Late Modern Age. Stanford, CA: Stanford University Press, 1924.

[80] Glaab, C. N. & Brown, A. T. A History of Urban America. New York: Macmillan Company, 1983.

[81] Glaser, B. G. and A. L. Strauss. The Discovery of Grounded Theory. Chicago: Aldine, 1967.

[82] Glazer, I. R. Philadelphia Theaters: A Pictorial Architectural History. Philadelphia: Athenaeum of Philadephia: New York: Dover Publications, 1994.

[83] Gray, B., & Hay, T. M. Political Limits to Interorganizational Consensus and Change. Journal of Applied Behavioral Science, 1986 (22): 95 – 112.

[84] Gray, B. Collaborating: Finding Common Ground for Multiparty Problems. San Francisco: Jossey – Bass, 1989.

[85] Gray, B. Conditions Facilitating Interorganizational Collaboration. Human Relations, 1985 (38): 911 –936.

[86] Grodach, & Silver. The Politics of Urban Cultural Policy: Global Perspectives. New York: Routledge, 2012.

[87] Hall, C. Rethinking Collaboration and Partnerships: A Public Policy Perspective. Journal of Sustainable Tourism, 1997 (7): 274 –289.

[88] Hall, P. The Key to Creativity, Excerpt from Cities in Civilization in the Intercultural City Reader, London: Comedia, 1998.

[89] Haviland. The Condition of Post – Modernity: An Inquiry into the Origins of Cultural Change. Oxford: Blackwell, 1989.

[90] Hayward, K. Responsible and Responsive Tourism Planning in the Community. Tourism Management, 1988, 9 (2): 105 –118.

[91] Hilary Anne Frost – Kumpf. Cultural Districts: Arts Management and Urban Redevelopment. A Thesis in Geography, Doctor of Philosophy. The Pennsylvania State University, 2001.

[92] Hitters, E. and G. Richards, The Creation and Management of Cultural Clusters, Creativity and Innovation Management, 2002, 11 (4): 234 –247.

[93] Hodos, J. I. Globalization, Regionalism, and Urban Restructuring: The Case of Philadelphia. Urban Affairs Review, 2002, 37 (3): 358 –379.

[94] Howard Becker. Sociological Work: Method and Substance. Chicago: Aldine, 1970.

[95] Huang Bin. An Evolution Study of Cultural & Creative Industries' Space in Beijing. Degree of Doctor of Philosophy, 2014.

[96] Huberman, A. M. and Miles, M. B. Data Management and Analysis Methods. In N. Denzin and Y. Linconln (Eds.). Handbook for Qualitative Research. Thousand Oaks, CA: Sage, 1994.

[97] Inman, R. How to Have a Fiscal Crisis: Lessons from Philadelphia. The American Economic Review, 1995, 85 (2): 378 –383.

[98] Jachson, & Cabois Sahel Rui. Artist Space Development: Making the Case and Assessing Impacts. Boston: Leveraging Investment in Creativity, 2006.

[99] Jackson, Maria Rosario. Arts and Cultural Participation Through a Neighborhood Lens. In the arts in a New Millennium: Research and Arts Sector (Eds.). Da-

vid Packrats and Valerie B. Morris. Westport, CT: Greenwood Publishing Group, 2003.

[100] Jackson, M. - R., J. Herranz, and F. Kabwasa - Green. Art and Culture in Communities: Systems of Support. Policy Brief No. 3 of the Culture, Creativity and Communities Program. Washington, DC: Urban Institute, 2003.

[101] Jamal, B. T., & Getz, D. Collaboration Theory and Community Tourism Planning. Annals of Tourism Research, 1995, 22 (1): 186 – 204.

[102] Jamal, B. T., & Stronza, A. Collaboration Theory and Tourism Practice in Protected Areas: Stakeholders, Structuring and Sustainability. Journal of Sustainable Tourism, 2009, 17 (2): 169 – 189.

[103] Jin Wenting. A Comparative Study on the Art & Culture Districts Under the Post – modern Cultural Context. A Thesis for the Degree of PHD, in the Anthropology of Art. China Art Research Institution, 2014.

[104] Joppe, M. Sustainable Community Tourism Development Revisited. Tourism Management, 1996, 17 (7): 475 – 479.

[105] Kaplan, S. M. Arts Park Concept Designed for Failure. Los Angeles Times, 1989 (25).

[106] Kay, J. H. Coins and Culture. In K. W. Green (Eds.). The City as a Stage: Strategies for the Arts in Urban Economics. Washington, DC: Partners for Livable Places, 1983.

[107] Kicker, W. J. M. Complexity, Governance and Dynamics: Conceptual Explorations of Public Network Management. In J. Kooiman (Eds.). Modern Governance. London: Sage, 1995.

[108] Kicker, W. J. M. Introduction: A Management Perspective on Policy networks. In W. J. M. Kicker, E. - H. Klijn & J. F. M. Koopenjan (Eds.). Managing Complex Networks: Strategies for the Public Sector. London: Sage, 1997.

[109] Klijn, E. - H., Koppenjan, J. F. M., & Termeer, C. J. A. M. Managing Networks in the Public Sector: A Theoretical Study of Management Strategies in Policy Networks. Public Administration, 1995, 73 (3): 437 – 454.

[110] Larson, M., & Wikstrom, E., Organinsing Events: Managing Conflict and Consensus in a Political Market Square. Event Management, 2004 (7): 51 – 65.

[111] Latour, B. Aramis: Or the Love of Technology. Brighton: Harvester Wheat Sheaf, 1996.

[112] Latour, B. Reassembling the Social: An Introduction to Actor – network –

References

theory. Oxford: Clarendon, 2005.

[113] Latour, B. Science in Action: How to Follow Scientists and Engineers through Society. Cambridge, MA: Harvard University Press, 1987.

[114] Laurie, B. , & Schmitz, M. Manufacturing and Productivity: The Making of an Industrial Base: 1850 – 1880. In T. Hershberg (Eds.) . Philadelphia: Work, Space, Family and Group Experience in the Nineteenth Century. New York: Oxford University Press, 1981.

[115] Lazzeretti, L. City of Art as a HC Local System and Cultural Destructuralization Processes. The Cluster of Art – restoration in Florence, International Journal of Urban and Regional Research, 2003, 27 (3): 635 –648.

[116] Lewis, J. Art, Culture and Enterprise, The Politics of Art and Cultural Industries, London: Rutledge, 1990.

[117] Lin, C. Y. , & Hsing, W. C. Culture – led Urban Regeneration and Community Mobilisation: The Case of the Taipei Bao – an Temple Area, Taiwan. Urban Studies, 2009, 46 (7): 1317 –1342.

[118] Liu Mingliang. 798 Cultural District: Research and Exploration under the Market Environment. Degree of Doctor of Philosophy, 2010.

[119] Lou Xiaoyan. The Study for Evolution of Industrial Heritage's Creative Cultural District. Thesis of Master Degree, Zhejiang Financing Institution, 2013.

[120] Malinowski. Cultural Clusters and the Post – industrial City: Towards the Remapping of Urban Cultural Policy. Urban Studies, 1992: 507 –532.

[121] Mark J. Stern and Susan C. Seifert. Cultural Clusters; the Implications of Cultural Assets Agglomeration for Neighborhood Revitalization. Journal of Planning Education and Research, 2010, 29 (3): 262 –279.

[122] Markusen, Ann, and Amanda Johnson. Artists' Centers: Evolution and Impact on Careers, Neighborhoods and Economies. With Christina Connelly, Andrea Martinez, Paul Singh and Galen Treuer. Minneapolis: University of Minnesota, Humphrey Institute of Public Affairs, Project on Regional and Industrial Economics, 2006.

[123] Martilla J. A. , James J. C. Importance Performance Analysis. Journal of Marketing, 1977, 41 (1): 77 –79.

[124] McLean, C. , & Hassard, J. Symmetrical Absence/Symmetrical Absurdity: Critical Notes on the Production of Actor – network Accounts. Journal of Management Studies, 2004, 41 (3): 492 –519.

[125]Medeiros de Araujo, L. , & Bramwell, B. Partnership and Regional Tourism

in Brazil. Annals of Tourism Research, 2002, 29 (4): 1138 – 1164.

[126] Menger, P. V He "ge" Monie Parisienne: E'conomieet Politique de La Gravitation Artistique. Geneva: International Institute for Labour Studies, 1993.

[127] Meyerson, K. E., Brooks, A., Lowell, J., & Zakaras, L. (Eds.). The Performing Arts in a New Era. Santa Monica: Rand Corp, 1978.

[128] Michela Arnaboldi, Nicola Spiller. Actor – network Theory and Stakeholder Collaboration: The Case of Cultural Districts. Tourism Management, 2001, 32 (2011): 641 – 654.

[129] Mitchell, R., K., Agle, B. R. & Wood, D. J. Toward a Theory of Stakeholder Identification and Salience: Defining the Principle of Who and What Really Counts. Academy of Management Review, 1997 (22): 853 – 886.

[130] Mommaas, H. Cultural Cluster and the Post – industrial City: Towards the Remapping of Unrban Cultural Policy. Urban Studies, 2004, 41 (3): 507 – 532.

[131] Montgomery, J. Cultural Quarters as Mechanisms for Urban Regeneration. Part I: Conceptualising Cultural Quarters. Planning, Practice & Research, 2003, 18 (4): 293 – 306.

[132] Mullins, P. Tourism Urbanization. International Journal of Urban and Regional Research, 1991, 15 (3): 326 – 342.

[133] Newman, P., & Smith, I. Cultural Production, Place, Politics on the South Bank of the Thames. International Journal of Urban and Regional Research, 2000, 24 (1): 9 – 24.

[134] Ogburn, W. F. The Folkways of a Scientific Sociology. Scientific Monthly, 1930 (30): 300 – 306.

[135] Oh H. Revisiting Importance – performance Analysis. Tourism Management, 2001, 22 (6): 617 – 627.

[136] Orum, A. M., Feagin, J. R., and Sjoberg, G. The Nature of the Case Study. In J. R. Feagin, A. M. Oru, & G. Sjoberg (Eds.). A Case for the Case Study. Chapel Hill, University of North Carolina Press, 1991.

[137] Parlett, M. and Hamilton, D. Evaluation as Illumination. In G. Glass (Ed.), Evaluation Studies Review Annual, 1976 (1): 140 – 157.

[138] Peretto, P., and M. Connolly. The Manhattan Metaphor. Journal of Economic Growth, 2007 (12): 329 – 350.

[139] Perlmutter, F. D., & Cnaan, R. A. Entrepreneurship in the Public Sector: The Horns of a Dilemma. Public Administration Review, 1995, 55 (1): 29 –

36.

[140] Peterson J. A. The City Beautiful Movement: Forgotten Origins and Lost Meanings. Journal of Urban History, 1976, 2 (4): 415-434.

[141] Pier Luigi Sacco, Guido Ferilli, Giorgio Tavano Blessi, and Massimiliano Nuccio, 2013.

[142] Pred, A. Urban Growth and the Circulation of Information: The United States System of Cities, 1790-1840. Cambridge, MA: Harvard University Press, 1973.

[143] Reid, S., & Arcodia, C. Understanding the Role of the Stakeholder in Event Management. In: Events and Place Making Conference Proceedings. Sydney: Australian Centre for Event Management, 2002.

[144] Richardson, J. J. (Eds.). Policy Styles in Western Europe. London: Allen and Unwin, 1982.

[145] Ritchie, J. R. B. Crafting a Destination Vision. Putting the Concept of Resident Responsive Tourism into Practice. Tourism Management, 1993 (14): 379-389.

[146] Rivera M. A., Shani A. and Severt D. Perceptions of Service Attributes in a Religious Theme Site: An Importance-satisfaction Analysis. Journal of Heritage Tourism, 2009, 4 (3): 227-243.

[147] Rossman, G., & Rallis, S. Learning in the Field. Thousand Oaks, CA: Sage, 1998.

[148] Ryan, C. Equity, Management, Power Sharing and Sustainability e Issues of the "New Tourism". Tourism Management, 2002 (23): 17-26.

[149] Sacco, P. L., Tavano Blessi, G., & Nuccio, M. Culture as an Engine of Local Development Processes: System-wide Cultural Districts. Working Paper. University IUAV of Venice, 2008.

[150] Santagata, W. Cultural Districts, Property Rights and Sustainable Economic Growth, International Journal of Urban and Regional Research, 2002, 1 (26): 9-23.

[151] Sautter, E. T., & Leisen, B. Managing Stakeholders; A Tourism Planning Model. Annals of Tourism Research, 1999, 26 (2): 312-328.

[152] Sayer, A. Method in Social Science. London: Routledge, 1992.

[153] Scranton, P. Proprietary Capitalism: The Textile Manufacture at Philadelphia, 1885-1900. Philadelphia: Temple University Press, 1983.

[154] Se Hoo Park. Can We Implant an Artist Community? A Reflection on Government-led Cultural Districts in Korea, 2015.

[155] Sheehan, L. R., & Ritchie, J. R. B. Destination Stakeholders Exploring Identity and Salience. Annals of Tourism Research, 2005, 32 (3): 711–734.

[156] Silberberg, T. Cultural Tourism and Business Opportunities for Museums and Heritage Sites. Tourism Management, 1995, 16 (5): 361–365.

[157] Skaler, R. M. Images of America: Philadelphia's Broad Street South and North. Charleston: Arcadia, 2003.

[158] Smith S. and Costello C., Culinary Tourism: Satisfaction with a Culinary Event Utilizing Importance Performance Grid Analysis. Journal of Vacation Marketing, 2009, 15 (2): 99–110.

[159] Stake, R. E. The Art of Case Study Research. Thousand Oaks, CA: Sage, 1995.

[160] Staler, R. M. Images of America: Philadelphia's Broad Street South and north. Charleston: Arcadia, 2003.

[161] Steffensen-Bruce I. A. Marble Palaces, Temples of Art: Art Museums, Architecture, and American Culture, 1890–1930. Lewisburg, PA: Bucknell University Press, 1998.

[162] Stern, M. J., & Seifert, S. C. Culture and Neighborhood Revitalization: A Harvest Document. Philadelphia: The Reinvestment Fund, 2007.

[163] Stoker, G. Regime Theory and Urban Politics. In D. Judge, G. Stoker, & H. Wolman (Eds.). Theories of Urban Politics. London: Sage, 1995.

[164] Strom, E. Cultural Coalitions: Past and Present. Paper Presented at the Urban Affairs Association Annual Meeting. Los Angeles, 2000.

[165] Thayer, T. Town into City (1746–1765). In R. F. Weigley, N. B. Wainwright, &E. Wolf 2 and (Eds). Philadelphia: A 300-Year Histoty (68–108). New York: W. W. Norton & Company, 1982.

[166] Tinkcom, H. M. The Revolutionary City, 1765–1783. In R. F. Weigley, N. B. Wainwright, & E. Wolf 2nd (Eds). Philadelphia: A 300-Year Histoty. New York: W. W. Norton & Company, 1982.

[167] Tonge J. and Moore S. A. Importance-satisfaction Analysis for Marine-park Hinterlands: A Western Australian Case Study. Tourism Management, 2007, 28 (3): 768–776.

[168] Tosun, C. Limits to Community Participation in the Tourism Development

References

Process in Developing Countries. Tourism Management, 2000 (21): 613 – 633.

[169] Tosun, C. Roots of Unsustainable Tourism Development at the Local Level: The case of Urgup in Turkey. Tourism Management, 1998 (19): 595 – 610.

[170] Trist, E. L. Referent Organization and the Development of Interorganizational Domains. Human Relations, 1983 (36): 247 – 268.

[171] U. S. Census Bureau. City and County Data Book 1950. Washington, DC: U. S. Department of Commerce: Author, 1952.

[172] U. S. Census Bureau. City and County Data Book 1970. Washington, DC: U. S. Department of Commerce: Author, 1972.

[173] Vernon, J. , Essex, S. , Pinder, D. , & Curry, K. Collaborative Policy Making. Local Sustainable Projects. Annals of Tourism Research, 2005, 32 (2): 325 – 345.

[174] Warner, C. van. Dimensions and Types of Networks. European Journal of Political Research, 1990, 21 (1 – 2): 241 – 261.

[175] Weiss, R. S. Alternative Approaches in the study of Complex Situations. Human Organization, 1996 (25): 198 – 206.

[176] Whyte, W. F. Street Corner Society: The Structure of an Italian Slum. Chicago: University of Chicago, 1943.

[177] Williams, R. Keywords. Oxford: Oxford University Press, 1985.

[178] Wilson, W. The City Beautiful Movement. Baltimore: Johns Hopkins University Press, 1989.

[179] Wolf, S. G. The Bicentennial City, 1968 – 1982. In R. E. Weigley, N. B. Wainwright, & E. Wolf 2nd (Eds) . Philadelphia: A 300 – Year History. New York: W. W. Norton & Company, 1982.

[180] Won Bae Kim. The Viability of Cultural Districts in Seoul. City, Culture and Society, 2011 (2): 141 – 150.

[181] Xiao Yanfei. Dynamic Mechanism and Innovation Models of Development of Economic Spaces of Creative Industrial District. Degree of Doctor of Philosophy, 2007.

[182] Yin, R. K. Case Study Research: Design and Methods (Newbury Park, CA: Sage), 1994.

[183] Zhang H. Q. and Chow I. Application of Importance – performance Model in Tour Guides' Performance: Evidence from Mainland Chinese Outbound Visitors in Hong Kong. Tourism Management, 2004, 25 (1): 81 – 91.

[184] Zhang Lingyun. Exploring Stakeholders of Culture Districts in Western Countries—Stratford as a Case in Canada. A Thesis for PHD History & Culture Institution Shandong University, 2012.

[185] Zhang Tianyu. Research for Song Village Art Ecology of Community. Degree of Doctor of Philosophy, 2013.

[186] Zhang Wang. The Study for Development Pattern of Creative Cultural Industrial in China. A Thesis for PHD Nanjing University, 2011.

[187] Zonabend, F. The Monograph in European Ethnology. Current Sociology, 1992, 40 (1): 49 -54.

[188] Zukin, S. The Cultures of Cities, Cambridge, MA: Blackwell, 1995.